THE CITY OF THE DEAD

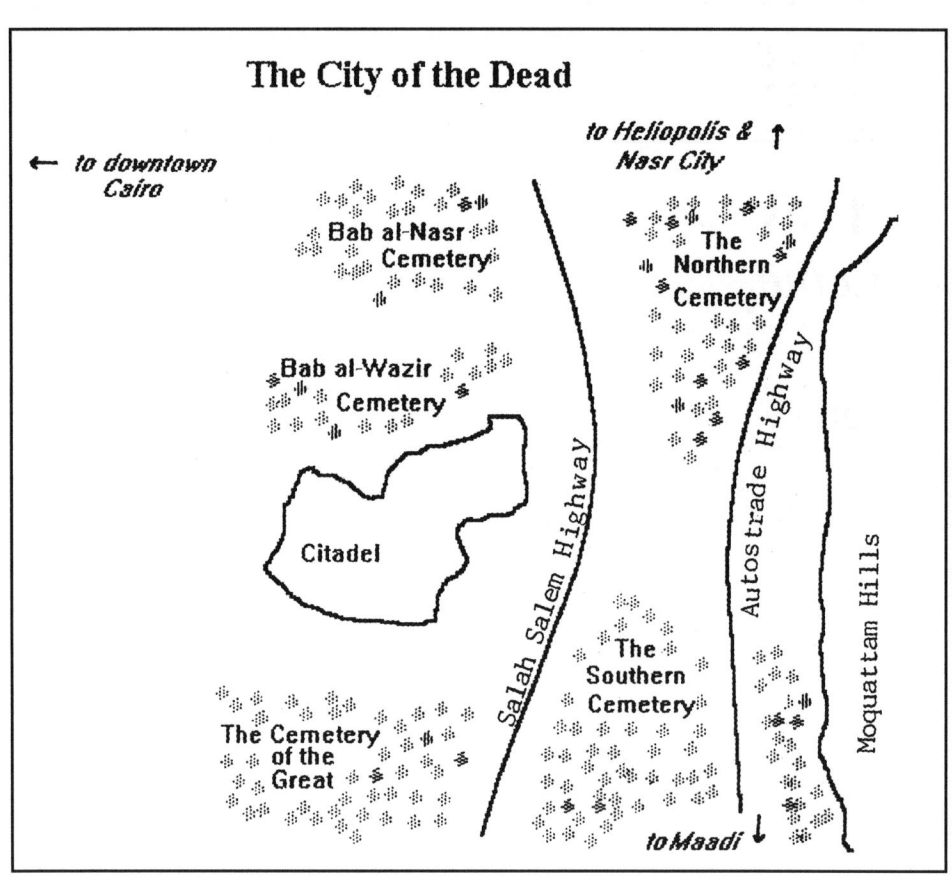

THE CITY OF THE DEAD

A History of Cairo's Cemetery Communities

Jeffrey A. Nedoroscik

BERGIN & GARVEY
Westport, Connecticut • London

Library of Congress Cataloging-in-Publication Data

Nedoroscik, Jeffrey A., 1970–
　　The city of the dead : a history of Cairo's cemetery communities / Jeffrey A. Nedoroscik.
　　　　p.　cm.
　　Includes bibliographical references and index.
　　ISBN 0–89789–533–9 (alk. paper)
　　1. Poor—Egypt—Cairo.　2. Cairo (Egypt)—Social conditions.
　　3. Cemeteries—Egypt—Cairo.　I. Title.
　　HV4159.C34N43　1997
　　305.569′0962′16—dc21　　　　97–10409

British Library Cataloguing in Publication Data is available.

Copyright © 1997 by Jeffrey A. Nedoroscik

All rights reserved. No portion of this book may be reproduced, by any process or technique, without the express written consent of the publisher.

Library of Congress Catalog Card Number: 97–10409
ISBN: 0–89789–533–9

First published in 1997

Bergin & Garvey, 88 Post Road West, Westport, CT 06881
An imprint of Greenwood Publishing Group, Inc.

Printed in the United States of America

The paper used in this book complies with the Permanent Paper Standard issued by the National Information Standards Organization (Z39.48–1984).

10　9　8　7　6　5　4　3　2　1

*For the residents of the City of the Dead
whose stories are told here,
and for my mother who
encouraged me to tell them*

Contents

Preface		ix
Acknowledgments		xiii
Introduction		1
1	The Physical and Social Growth of the Cemeteries	11
	Stories: Zeinab Ali—*Life's Wisdom*	28
	Zekia Imbabi—*Village without Fields*	33
	Fatima Ali—*The Black Sheep*	37
2	The Modern Era: Informal Housing in the City of the Dead	41
	Stories: Ashrof Mohamed—*Sir*	78
	Arabe—*His Generation*	81
	Mamdouh Abbass—*My First and True Home*	84
	Mohamed—*Life, Politics and Sophia Loren*	92
3	The Future of the City of the Dead	97
	Stories: Salah Mohamed—*The Cleopatra Salesman*	104
	Mohamed Mousa—*Hatred of Life and of the Living*	106
	Fardoos Ahmed—*Hell on Earth*	108

Conclusion	115
Glossary of Arabic Terms	123
Notes	125
Selected Bibliography	129
Index	133

Preface

> [To] get to know this great city [Cairo], you must have time on your hands, for only to the loiterer and the wanderer are her intimate beauties revealed.
> —Russell, *Medieval Cairo and the Monasteries of Wadi Natrun*

In 1990 I was given a grant from the College of the Holy Cross (Worcester, Mass.) and the Sutton, Massachusetts Arts Council to spend a semester studying in Egypt. During my time there I tried to assimilate as much as possible into Egyptian society. When I wasn't in my classes at the American University in Cairo, I spent a lot of time walking the streets of Cairo, observing the city, meeting people from all parts of society, and trying to understand the culture. I enjoyed friendships with the students and professors at the university, but I also wanted to meet Egyptians from other, more traditional ranks of society. It was on the streets of Cairo that I met an Egyptian man from the City of the Dead. I eventually began tutoring him in English.

These English lessons were held in a tomb-home in the Southern Cemetery of the City of the Dead at the base of the Moquattam Hills. It was there that I saw a community of poor but proud and resourceful people, who, despite the odds, were eking out an existence on the fringes of society. I was fascinated and intrigued by these people living among the dead.

I related my experiences in the City of the Dead to a prominent anthropologist at the American University in Cairo. She commented on the unlikeliness of the situation I had become involved in. She said that life in the City of the Dead had not been well documented because class differences prevented researchers, such as herself, from being accepted into the society of the "dead." A literature search on the subject quickly revealed that she was right. There is little written on the City of the Dead beyond brief descriptions of the famous monuments and tombs of Islam that it possesses.

I left Egypt, after my brief stay, with a desire to return to further experience its life, culture, and traditions. The Thomas J. Watson Foundation, named in honor of the founder of the IBM Corporation, funds a year of independent study and travel for sixty ambitious graduates of certain colleges from across the United States each year. I was honored to receive such a fellowship in 1992, which paved the way for my return to Egypt. I spent a year traveling around the country exploring tombs and temples, mosques and monasteries, generally "things" Egyptian. The most rewarding and fascinating experiences, however, continued to be those within the borders of the City of the Dead—experiences that gave me a broad understanding of the community of the City of the Dead, and which provoked me to write this book.

Upon my return to Egypt, I had intended to live in the City of the Dead. However, after suffering from dysentery and having been warned that a foreigner living in the City of the Dead would not be accepted by Egypt's government, I decided to make my permanent residence outside the City's borders. Still, over the next two years, I would be a frequent visitor to the cemeteries. I would speak, laugh, cry, play, eat, and even sleep among the people of the City of the Dead.

In my excursions to the cemeteries, I investigated and familiarized myself with the long history of the burial grounds that form the City. I toured the major monuments of the cemeteries and spent hours upon hours in libraries to discover their religious, historical, and architectural significance. Through the relationships that I formed, I was able to grasp the complexities of the people and culture forming the modern-day City of the Dead. I was a frequent visitor to numerous tomb-homes, where I was received with genuine kindness and curiosity. Soon, one family began referring to me as their son and brother and even gave me an adopted name, Ismail Abbass. They didn't want me to return to my home in the States. I had a new home.

As these various families became more and more comfortable with my presence in their cemetery world, I ceased to be a guest in their eyes. Instead, I became like a member of their extended family. This allowed me to view the day-to-day activities of the household in their natural form. I was no longer given the special attention of a visitor—cushions were no longer placed at my seat at mealtime, utensils were no longer brought out for me to eat with, and I was no longer given the largest portions at meals. Rather, I participated in and observed their activities in pure form.

As I became more of a fixture in the City of the Dead community, I was allowed more freedom to explore other areas and aspects of the City of the Dead. At first, people I met were reluctant to talk about the area beyond their tomb-home, and they discouraged me from venturing into the cemeteries. I am not sure if they wished to protect me from any harm that they thought might befall a foreigner drifting through the City of the Dead, or if they simply hoped to keep me to themselves (by having a foreigner in their house, their status was raised in the eyes of other members of the community). Still, I insisted on meeting others.

The people of the City of the Dead proved to be just as curious about me as I was about them. They questioned me about my religion and about life in the United States. They asked me how I could possibly leave my family and travel 5,000 miles across the globe. They wondered why I was not married yet, and they always volunteered to find me a good Egyptian bride.

I was fascinated with my interactions with these people. I recorded all of my experiences and observations in a journal that forms the basis of this book, together with historical research as well as comparisons with other studies of poor communities in Cairo and other parts of the developing world. Some of these works were instrumental in helping me to recognize and understand what I was witnessing.

My study was helped significantly by another relationship that I formed outside of the City of the Dead. I befriended an Egyptian man who is from a small village in the Nile Delta region of Egypt. I have spent a great deal of time at his home, and I have been able to observe and participate in the day-to-day life of rural Egyptians. Because most of the residents of the City of the Dead are rural-to-urban migrants to Cairo, my time in the Egyptian countryside became important. I was able to better understand the process of rural-to-urban migration as well as the similarities between life in the City of the Dead and rural Egypt. I learned what qualities and values migrants to the city keep, and how they adjust to their new urban environment.

My familiarity with rural Egypt was particularly helpful in understanding the women of the City of the Dead. When I first began my study, I was afraid that I would not learn enough about the women's world. It was in this area, however, that being a foreigner actually seems to have benefited me the most. As a non-Egyptian male, I was actually given more freedom to join in the activities of women, and much of my time in the cemeteries took place during the morning hours when the men were away from the tombs. I did not have to go off and work—I was allowed to sit in the tomb-homes with the women. I participated in their conversations and observed their daily tasks. The same was true of my visits to the Egyptian countryside. As a result, I feel that I have a good understanding of the dynamics of the lives of women in the City.

My initial stay in the City of the Dead lasted for one year as I had to leave Egypt in June of 1993 when the money for my fellowship had long run out and I had drained my personal finances. Leaving proved to be difficult. I still felt that there was so much more for me to experience in Egypt. Fortunately, I was able to find work that quickly returned me to Cairo, and I now work as a contractor for the United States Agency for International Development's (USAID) mission in Cairo. Throughout my work, the City of the Dead has remained a part of my life.

Ironically, everyday on my way to work I take a shortcut through the Northern Cemetery of the City of the Dead. Even now, I am amazed by its existence. Every day, my eyes search the landscape of the cemetery for some sign of change. I look into the eyes of the residents sitting in their doorways, and I search to see some glimmer of hope. Change, however, is coming slow to the City of the Dead . . . but I will keep watching.

ACKNOWLEDGMENTS

It was through the efforts and support of many people that my experiences in Egypt, and this resulting literary work, were made possible. I would like to express my fondest gratitude and appreciation. Had the wonderful people at the Thomas J. Watson Foundation not thought that I would take full advantage of the fellowship year to enjoy an incredible cultural and educational experience, my time spent in the City of the Dead might still be a distant dream. The encouragement of two talented scholars, mentors, and friends, Dr. Selma Botman and the late Dr. Maurizio Vannicelli, as well as other members of the academic community of the College of the Holy Cross provided a constant inspiration. To my family whose support was never-ending, I dedicate this to you. I sincerely thank El Sayed (Essam) Mohamed for his assistance in translations and for letting me drag him to places that he never would have dreamed of going. I would also like to thank Jennifer Notkin, Connie Paraskeva, Dr. Susan Davis, Elizabeth Fernea, and Dr. Robert Fernea for commenting on the manuscript as well as Simon O'Rourke. Most important, however, I have to thank the many residents of the City of the Dead who welcomed me into their homes and hearts. I hope that some good can be accomplished by making your stories known.

THE CITY OF THE DEAD

INTRODUCTION

> In most civilizations the houses of the dead are more magnificent than the houses of the living.
>
> —Ragan, *Space of Death*

The City of the Dead is a complex area of Cairo that most Cairenes are aware of but few understand. The task of this book is to provide an overview of the historical evolution of the City of the Dead, focusing on the modern-day circumstances of the cemeteries as an area of informal housing for hundreds of thousands of Egypt's urban poor. Primary to this goal is understanding how the City of the Dead came to house these masses of people as well as looking at the different facets of the lives of the people of the cemeteries. What the future holds for this unique community and its people will also be addressed, and an analysis of what the City of the Dead represents in terms of a historical and cultural phenomenon will be presented. Moreover, this book will offer an appraisal of how the cemetery communities relate to the development challenges facing Egypt.

WHAT IS THE CITY OF THE DEAD?

Contrary to its name, you will find the City of the Dead to be very much alive as you attempt to make your way through the giant, complex labyrinth. The City is actually a group of vast cemeteries stretching across some five square miles of Cairo, the largest metropolis in the Arab world. They are not cemeteries in the conventional Western sense, with burial plots six feet deep and gravestones marking the burial sites. Although this type of grave does exist in the City of the Dead, the majority of the burial sites consist of permanent above ground structures (sometimes as large as houses) built upon large, underground tombs.

Traditionally, when Egyptians bury their dead there is an extensive mourning period (about forty days). During this period, according to Cairene tradition, the family of the deceased frequently live in a room or rooms built up around the tomb where the deceased family member is buried. In modern times, because of structural underdevelopment so common in Egypt, many of these rooms have become temporary or permanent homes for many of Cairo's urban poor.

Cairo suffers from a severe and chronic lack of adequate and affordable housing. Indeed, the housing crisis is characteristic of much of the developing world. A metropolitan area of more than fifteen million inhabitants, Cairo is deficient in affordable housing. For Cairo's urban poor—this group includes recent immigrants as well as more established city dwellers—shelter is a luxury rather than a right. Because Cairo is so inhospitable to the indigent, many have resorted to survival outside of the law in the so-called informal sector. (The informal sector consists of activities that are not offically recognized through registration and taxation procedures.) Like Lima, Peru, Calcutta, India, and other cities of the developing world, Cairo has proven incapable of providing a decent quality of life for its poor within the system.

In Cairo, the closest that most people come to the City of the Dead is in a speeding car on Salah Salim Highway. The highway offers a vantage point from which vast areas of the cemeteries can be observed. Few people who ride by the City of the Dead dare to wander inside. From the highway, the City of the Dead appears to be orderly and common. It blends into the landscape. It is possible to pass by the vast Muslim necropolises time and time again and fail to acknowledge their existence. Indeed, looking down upon the City of the Dead from the blacktop lanes of Salah Salim, one would hardly guess the complex nature of the cemeteries.

Throughout history, travelers and scholars have recorded their initial impressions of the City of the Dead:

> From a distance the cities of the dead appear as a forest of minarets and domes.
> (Napoleon, *Description De L'Egypte*, 1987)

Introduction

The huge domes and minaretted tombs of the Mamluke beys, standing in the desert outside of the walls of Cairo, are also an architectural triumph of their kind, and not even the dust and squalor of the slums that now surround them or the hordes of ragged children who haunt this city of the dead, can quite obscure the revelation that there was a vision here that rose above the barbarous and material life. (Mooerhead, *The Blue Nile*, 1982)

From the air the funeral fringe demonstrates a familiar rectangular and regular street plan with what appears to be an orderly procession of detached but roofless bungalows, a travesty on suburbia. Its openness and order are even more conspicuous in contrast with the crazy-quilt confusion of medieval Cairo which it adjoins. Coming down to earth, one exits from the bustling crowds of the medieval city into the dusty but straight and wide streets of the cemetery as if one had blundered upon a surrealistic stage set. (Abu-Lughod, *Cairo: 1001 Years of the City Victorious*, 1971)

[The City of the Dead] did not seem inviting. It has the look of a bidonville—hot, dusty, dilapidated, with a quantity of domes. (Hagg, *Guide to Cairo*, 1985)

[T]he Northern Cemetery is a bleak and foreboding place, lying at the foot of the Moquattam Hills—sere and dusty, a jumble of small houses with innumerable domes rising among them. (Parker, Sabin & Williams, *Islamic Monuments in Cairo: A Practical Guide*, 1985)

All of Cairo's great Muslim necropolises, which combine to form the City of the Dead, lie to the east of the modern downtown area. Salah Salim Highway severs the City of the Dead into different parts that were once organically joined. The City is made up of numerous cemeteries: the Cemetery of the Great is to the south of Salah al-Din's majestic Citadel and lies mostly on the west side of Salah Salim. This cemetery runs along the ancient aqueduct that once brought water from the Nile to the Citadel. The Southern Cemetery is on the other side of the highway, opposite the Cemetery of the Great. It extends from the eastern entrance of the Citadel to the outskirts of the modern Cairo suburb of El Maadi. It is bordered on one side by Salah Salim and on the other side by the steep slopes of the Moquattam Hills. The Northern Cemetery begins at the north-east corner of the Citadel and extends northward to the boundaries of Nasr City, another of Cairo's modern suburbs. Salah Salim Highway runs along its border to the west, while the Autostrade Highway and the Moquattam Hills flank the cemetery to the east. Across Salah Salim from the Northern Cemetery lies the Bab al-Nasr Cemetery, which extends from the ancient Fatimid gate of the same name out toward Army Square and Abbassia. Finally, wrapping around toward the front of the Citadel, and on the west side of Salah Salim, is the Bab al-Wazir Cemetery.

Looking down upon the City of the Dead, the eye meets a tapestry of square and rectangular interlocked buildings interspersed with the major monuments. The buildings are separated by wide avenues in some areas and dusty paths in others. In some areas the buildings are arranged in neatly planned rows. In other areas the structures are hodgepodge, lacking any discernible direction or design.

Tombs typically consist of a permanent structure that includes one or more rooms and a walled courtyard (*howsh*). The number and size of the rooms of the individual family tombs reflect the wealth, power, and social status of the families. Magnificent old family tomb complexes sit beside newer, more poorly constructed tombs. Older tombs are typically made of stone. Newer ones are constructed of bricks covered with plaster. There are also self-assembled wooden and aluminum sheds, which generally house only the living and not the dead. Some tombs are merely four thin walls built around a barren courtyard. Other complexes contain numerous rooms built out of the finest materials. Many of them are quite spacious and were designed to allow the family of the deceased to come for extended visits. The rooms may have roofs over them to provide shelter for visiting family members, and they may be extensively furnished for the comfort of family members during such visits. Accommodations for these family stays were an integral part of the design of the tombs.

The permanent structures of the cemeteries demanded caretakers or guardians whose accommodations were also provided for. The tomb keepers and watchmen, along with their families, formed the first communities of the City of the Dead.

Some tombs contain gardens in the courtyards and have beautifully crafted cenotaphs or grave stones marking the grave sites. Walls are often richly decorated and varying qualities and quantities of doors and gates are used to allow some people in and to keep others out. Over the years, however, as the tombs have been invaded by the city's poor, these barriers have increasingly failed to serve their purpose. Homeless squatters have gained or forced entry into the mausolea.

The dead are typically interred in underground tombs built beneath the floor of the family's rooms or below the courtyards. Gravestones mark the burial site. The underground cavities are large or small, depending on the family they are serving, and will have a single opening by which they can be entered. The tombs are re-opened and closed upon each subsequent family member's death. Most family burial areas have one room in which the male members of the family are buried and another in which the female members are laid to rest. Larger complexes of wealthier families may have separate rooms or tombs for single family members, especially if these individuals were prominent in the family or in society.

The opening of the tomb is typically covered over by a few stone slabs, which are concealed by a thin layer of dirt. When the dirt and the stone slabs are removed, a set of stairs leading down into the chamber is revealed. Upon these stairs, the body, which has undergone the rites of a Muslim burial, is brought into the tomb and laid to rest.

The location of the opening of the tomb is often not noticeable to an outsider but is well-known by family members. Indeed, they have all seen it when they have gathered at funerals. Many of them have walked inside to say their final good-byes. In the traditional Muslim funeral process, the rites of ablution are performed on the dead body while the Qu'ran is being read. The body is then dried and pieces of cloth are stitched and wrapped around it, secured at the head and legs. The body is transferred to a wooden bier and covered with a shawl. The bier is carried with the chants and whispers of "There is no God but Allah." The body is usually taken to a mosque where it is placed at the prayer niche (*mihrab*) while funeral prayers are recited until the body is brought to the cemetery.

At the cemetery, the mouth of the grave has already been opened and any unbound bones of past family members that may have escaped their decaying shrouds have been collected and returned to their shrouds.* The walls of the tomb have been painted with lime (especially is the tomb if new; the lime helps to absorb moisture in the tomb cavity), and henna has been mixed with the sand of the grave's floor in preparation for the new body.** The corpse is brought into the tomb and the burial shroud is cut. The head lays facing Mecca and has found its eternal earthly home.

The dead are frequently visited by family members on their birthdays and during religious holidays and feasts, particularly during *Ramadan* (the Muslim holy month that commemorates the revelation of the Qu'ran to the Prophet Muhammed). One historical account offers this explanation of visits to the dead: "When the people of Cairo wish to go in for serious dissipation they visit the graves of their relations, and then, in hours

---

*According to Egyptian burial practices, the body is buried shrouded but not in a coffin.
**The use of henna dates to Pharaonic times. Placing henna under the deceased was believed to help facilitate the person's passage into Paradise.

expressly reserved for cheerful mourners, they listen to the chanting of the holy book."[1]

The traditional Egyptian attitude toward cemeteries greatly differs from conventional Western attitudes. Historically, Egyptians refuse to see the graveyard as a dark, evil, and forbidden place. No atmosphere of fear or danger surrounded the cemetery. The cemetery has always been an active part of the community. Only in recent times have more Western views of cemeteries pervaded Egyptian attitudes. Indeed, it appears that it was not until the French occupation (from 1798 to 1801) that the idea of a strict separation between tombs and houses was introduced into Egyptian culture. This view was reinforced under British occupation. Today, those living in the cemeteries are ostracized from mainstream society.

This book takes a historical look at the development of the City of the Dead from its humble beginnings to present day. In particular it focuses on the economic, social, and practical life of people on the margins of subsistence. It looks at the physical expansion of the cemeteries, important buildings and monuments, the use of the cemetery city as informal housing, and the backgrounds of the tomb-dwellers. It documents the lives of some of the inhabitants of the City of the Dead in order to portray their economic activities, their educational opportunities, their social activities, their access to health care and other services, their relationship with the world outside of the City of the Dead, and other aspects of their day-to-day existence. Particular attention has been paid to gender and an understanding of how men, women, and children interact and participate in the family economy. The relationship between the government and the people of the City of the Dead is also examined with special attention paid to crime, harassment, the use of utilities, and visions of the future.

Chapter 1 looks at the physical and social growth of the cemeteries from their beginnings as a few humble tombs in the desert more than 1,200 years ago. It traces the cemeteries' physical and social development through the various periods of Egyptian history beginning with the Arab conquest of Egypt up through the era of Ottoman rule. This historical overview demonstrates how the City of the Dead closely reflects the evolution of Cairo itself. Throughout this overview, many of the major monuments of the City of the Dead—mosques, tombs, and Islamic schools—are identified, and their significance in Egypt's history as well as to modern day Egypt is explored. Indeed, some of the most magnificent and renowned monuments of the Islamic world are located in the City of the Dead, making the cemeteries an area of significant historical importance. Chapter 1 also demonstrates how life in the cemeteries is not only a contemporary phenomenon. The City of the Dead has always been an active part of the community of Cairo, and there have always been people living, working, and carrying out various other activities among the tombs.

Chapter 1 builds the foundation for an exploration of the modern face of the City of the Dead, a situation where the cemeteries provide informal housing to hundreds of thousands of Egypt's urban poor. Chapter 2 attempts to provide an overall picture of life in the City of the Dead. From an investigation of the roots of the people living in the City of the Dead to an analysis of their day-to-day activities—economic activities, religious activities, educational opportunities, and access to adequate and affordable health care—to the social dynamics of family life in the cemetery communities (with particular emphasis on the experiences of women and children). In addition, the relationship between residents of the City of the Dead and formal Cairenes as well as their relationship with the Egyptian government and security forces is examined.

Chapter 3 looks at the uncertain future of these illegal cemetery communities. It reveals government plans to confiscate the tomb-dwellings of the cemeteries' squatters, relocate many of the tombs into the Egyptian desert, and use the valuable land upon which the City of the Dead rests for the development of business and tourism. Opposition to these plans is explored from the vantage point of three groups: tomb-dwellers, cemetery-plot owners, and scholars of religion, Islamic history and architecture.

Last, I offer my concluding remarks. These remarks focus on what the overall purpose of this book is: to provide a holistic view of the City of the Dead and offer readers a chance to see these curious informal cemetery communities not merely as problem areas (as so often is the circumstance), but for the complex neighborhoods that they are: informal communities that have been formed out of necessity. They are a symptom of the underlying structural problems facing Egypt; physical proof of an economy unable to provide a decent standard of living for millions of its disadvantaged. So often, it is easy to view these people of informal communities such as the City of the Dead as the problem, as a nuisance to society. These people, however, are struggling to survive in a system that has locked the doors to their very existence. They have been creative in their efforts, and they have provided shelter for themselves and their families outside of the formal system. They are not the problem. Rather, they are victims. Labeling these people as the problem leaves them nothing more than scapegoats for a society that is afraid to admit their own deep-lying deficiencies and the feeling of shared responsibility that would result.

Underlying this is the issue of problem-solving. I do not pretend to offer a solution. Such a task is beyond the scope of this book. Still, as long as the City of the Dead is seen as a problem by the government, the solution will be the cemeteries' ultimate destruction. However, if the problem is seen as one that is a combination of elements that lie much deeper in the structure of Egypt's economy, a more enduring solution can be found. Only then will the *need* for a community such as the City of the Dead cease to exist.

Throughout this book, the term poor is sometimes used to describe the people of the City of the Dead. This term is used, however, in the absence of a more accurate word to describe the economic situation of these people and their economic position vis-à-vis the larger urban population of Cairo. I feel the need to clarify the use of this word, as it is often used in a condescending manner. Even when used purely as a measure of economic status, the question arises, "Poor compared to who or according to whom?" Certainly, everyone has their own idea of what constitutes poverty. For many Westerners, anyone with an income under $9,000 per year is living in poverty. For many people of the developing world, $9,000 per year would be an enviable income.

According to Webster's Dictionary, poor is "(1) having little or no means of support; needy (2) lacking in some quality, specifically (a) inadequate (b) inferior or worthless (c) contemptible (3) worthy of pity; unfortunate." Thus, the many alternative meanings of this common word leave room for misunderstanding. By referring to the people of the City of the Dead as poor, I certainly do not mean to identify them as inferior, worthless, or inadequate in any way or form. Rather, I am referring to their economic situation as compared to others in the larger urban community, in terms of indicators such as income, nutritional level, access to shelter, access to health care, and educational opportunities. Therefore, the people of the City of the Dead are poor in that, given their incomes and their restricted access to such basic necessities as food and shelter, they often find themselves at a disadvantage relative to fellow Cairenes.

In addition to examining the City of the Dead as an area of informal housing, I offer the reader a chance to view these cemetery communities as areas of historical importance. The monuments and tombs that grace its surface represent more than a thousand years of history. They represent the unfolding of Egypt and explain how the Egypt of today grew from that of yesterday. It is a valuable archive for all Egyptians.

Foremost in achieving the goals outlined above is introducing the reader to the individuals who inhabit the City of the Dead. Interspersed throughout these pages are life stories of ten of the cemetery residents. These brief biographies talk about the lives, experiences, perspectives, and ideals of individuals and families of the City of the Dead's unique community. Men and women, old and young, and from different areas in the City of the Dead, those chosen provide a cross-section of the City's people.

No one can tell the stories of the residents as well as those who dwell in the tombs themselves. Therefore, I have attempted to paint a portrait of their lives and to write their stories as they would tell them. The people living in the cemeteries represent a variety of people with different attitudes, outlooks, and a wealth of life experiences. Yet, through various avenues, they have been joined together in a unique Cairo suburb: the City of the Dead.

1

THE PHYSICAL AND SOCIAL GROWTH OF THE CEMETERIES

> One mile away from Cairo is a city which is not walled, is as large as Venice, and has tall structures and short ones; in this city are buried all who die in Cairo.
> —Emmanual Piloti, 1420
> European traveler

The City of the Dead, both as a home for the living and for the dead, is not a new phenomenon. In fact, its history is as old as that of the city of Cairo itself. In many ways, Cairo's history can be traced through the physical and social development of the great cemeteries and the tombs they hold. The variety of people for whom the cemeteries serve as an eternal resting place, the architecture of the mausolea, as well as the living inhabitants of the modern-day City of the Dead all reflect Cairo's evolution. From Cairo's beginnings as a settlement on the east bank of the Nile, through its periods of eminence and grandeur, to its current status as an urban metropolis grown beyond its means, those five square miles at the base of the Moquattam Hills bear witness to the centuries of Cairo's history. In addition, a historical analysis of the City of the Dead shows that the cemeteries were always an active part of the community: home to guardians of the tombs, Qu'ran reciters, Sufi monks, the poor, the sick, and even criminals hiding from the law. These ancient burial grounds are also of great historical and religious importance to Islam and contain some of the most impressive and significant monuments of the Muslim world.

This chapter will provide the reader with a historical timeline of the City of the Dead's growth, both physically and socially. It will demonstrate how the cemeteries were expanded by each succeeding generation of Egypt's rulers as well as the social importance of the cemeteries throughout Cairo's history. Numerous monuments will be described in terms of their physical and artistic attributes as well as for the roles that these monuments played (and often continue to play) in Cairene society. From end to end, acre upon acre, mile after mile, the land of the City of the Dead not only provides an eternal resting place for an extraordinary number of dead and homes for countless living, it is also an invaluable archive, a chronicle of life and legacy. A walk through the City of the Dead is a walk through history itself.

THE ARAB CONQUEST 640 A.D.

The Southern Cemetery of the City of the Dead has served as a burial ground since the Arab conquest of Egypt in the seventh century. 'Amr ibn al-As led his Arab armies into Egypt in 640 A.D. and successfully subdued the pre-existing Coptic Christian community. Many of the Copts welcomed the Arabs in the hope that they would be kinder rulers than the Byzantines, who had previously controlled the land. Over time, many in the Christian community willingly or reluctantly converted to the new faith of Islam until, by the tenth century, the majority of the inhabitants of Egypt were Muslim. Copts often intermarried with the Arabs who migrated to Egypt to take advantage of the fertile soil of the Nile Valley. The young religion swept through Egypt, spreading its beliefs and message. In the process, Islam adapted to suit the culture and unique society of Egypt. More so than in any other facet of the new society that emerged, this adjustment became evident in burial practices. Egyptian Muslims adopted such characteristics of ancient Egypt as the belief in the afterlife and numerous funerary practices.

There are no pyramids filled with treasure in the City of the Dead or mummies of eternal rulers whose *ka* now roams the afterworld. There are, however, mausolea that are traditionally Egyptian. The Muslim invaders continued the practice of interring the dead as well as the practice of building residences in the areas of the tombs. The dead were buried in sealed underground tombs, which could be re-opened for future burials. In this way, generations of a family could be entombed in the same structure. In addition, living quarters to house family members during periods of mourn-

Physical Growth of the Cemeteries

ing and visits to the dead were frequently built adjacent to or near the tombs (a practice that is important to the City of the Dead's modern personality).

In traditional Islam there should be no screaming, no crying, no wearing of black, and no forty-day mourning period. Such practices are perceived as refusing to accept God's judgment. In Egypt, however, Islam adapted to death rites that are traditionally Egyptian and date as far back as Pharaonic times. For example, Egyptian Muslims observe a forty-day mourning period, which derives from the length of time it took the Pharaonic undertaker to purify the body and preserve it in natron (hydrated sodium carbonate). Also, modern Egyptians wrap their dead in white sheets in much the same way that mummies were wrapped, and wear black clothing in mourning.

The oldest tombs of the City of the Dead are located in the Southern Cemetery in an area known among English speakers as the "Cemetery of the Great" or, in Arabic, *Al-Ashriffiyya* (literally, Place of the Most Exalted Ones). This immense burial ground was used by the conquering Arabs, the Tulunids, the Fatimids, the Ayyubids, and on through the Mamluke era. It is there that the tomb of the Imam al-Shafi'i can be found. A mausoleum that illustrates the cemeteries' religious and historical importance as well as the way in which the City of the Dead has evolved to its present-day appearance.

The Imam al-Shafi'i was the founder of one of the four rites of Sunni Islam and claimed descent from Abu Talib, the uncle of the Prophet Muhammed. He studied in Medina and traveled to Yemen where he was active in a rebellion that brought him into disfavor with the Caliph Hawn al-Rachid. He later taught in Baghdad, where he developed ideas on Islamic jurisprudence that would become the Shafi'ite rite of Islam, to which most Egyptians adhere today. Cairo historian Gaston Wiet claims, "the role that he [the Imam al-Shafi'i] played in elaborating religious law is so important that it cannot be exaggerated, for he was truly the founder of methodology in the field of religious legislation."[2] The Iman al-Shafi'i eventually travelled to Egypt, where he lived until his death.

Although the Imam al-Shafi'i died in Egypt in 820 A.D., the present foundation of his tomb dates to 1211 A.D. and is the largest Muslim mortuary chamber in Egypt. The Imam was buried in the tomb area of the family of Sayyid Mohamed 'Abd al-Hakim. The mausoleum was built by al-Adil, brother of the famous Ayyubid leader Salah al-Din, and it includes the 'Abd al-Hakam family cemetery within its walls. The mausoleum is covered with a large bronze dome, which can be seen from outside the cemetery. The dome rises above the urban area that has been built up around the tomb over the years. Dating to 1722, the dome was the work of 'Ali Bey al-Kebir. It is made of two wooden shells, thirty centimeters apart, that are covered with lead and appear to be modelled after the Dome of the Rock in Jerusalem. At the dome's crest is a metal boat, which was designed to hold grain for birds. The boat is also a Pharaonic symbol, representing the vessel that carries the dead to the afterworld. Inside the mausoleum there are two *mihrabs* (niches that indicate the direction of Mecca that Muslims face when praying). The earlier one was not correctly in line with Mecca. The second one, in correct orientation, was a donation of the Mamluke Sultan Qaytbay.

Like other tombs in this area, al-Shafi'i's original mausoleum may have been a more simple burial chamber than the present-day structure. Over the centuries, however, more elaborate mausolea were built over many of the older tombs, some even containing mosques and Islamic schools (*madrasa*). The first of such schools in Egypt was founded by Salah al-Din al Ayyubi, and was built at the Shafi'i burial site. Salah al-Din, founder of the Ayyubid Dynasty in twelfth-century Egypt, built the school as part of his campaign to convert Egypt back from Shi'i Islam to Sunni Islam. Much like the Imam al-Shafi'i, he was a pioneer in Islamic education. His influence, too, can be seen throughout the City of the Dead's monuments.

In Sunni Islam, the Imam al-Shafi'i is esteemed as one of the great Muslim saints. As one of the City of the Dead's holiest shrines, his mausoleum attracts visitors from around the Muslim world who make *ziyyarah*, or visitation, to the tomb to recite prayers in al-Shafi'i's honor. Every year on the occasion of his birthday, a religious fair (*mulid*) is held at the tomb.

The Imam al-Shaffi'i's tomb is important in understanding the growth of the City of the Dead both physically and as an active part of the growing Muslim community of Cairo. For centuries, the tomb has been revered as a source of *baraka* or spiritual blessing. The sick travel here to be cured or to die at the mausoleum. Throughout history, the poor have settled around the tomb to seek the benevolence of visitors. Thus, the phenomenon of people living in the cemeteries is not new. It is not only in the face of the twentieth century's housing crisis that people have settled among the dead. People have been living there for centuries for various reasons. Janet Abu-Lughod writes:

> One should not imagine . . . that these cemeteries were (or are) used exclusively as burial sites. Although physically separated, they were never functionally segregated. From early times, among the shrines were found monasteries and schools for various religious and mystic orders. Some of

these served as free hostels for itinerant scholars or travelers. In addition, guarding each family tomb was a resident retainer and his dependents. To this population must be added a few temporary and permanent squatters who found the rent-free stone and wooden structures of the "tomb city" more spacious and substantial than the mudbrick huts available to them within the city proper. With such a resident population, it was perhaps inevitable that some artisans and shopkeepers should gravitate to the area to fulfill the demand for daily goods and services. Nor were these the only functions of this unique land use. Just as the marshlands provided open recreational space for the militaristic sports pursued by the Mamlukes, the Cities of the Dead provided recreational facilities for the bulk of the population who repaired there weekly and, in even greater numbers, on the major festivals occasions.[3]

In this way, life in the City of the Dead is as old as the City of the Dead itself.

A short distance from the tomb of the Imam al-Shafi'i, also in the Cemetery of the Great, is the mausoleum of 'Ogba ibn 'Amr. 'Amr, a friend of the Prophet Muhammed as well as a companion of 'Amr ibn al-As (leader of the Muslim invaders of Egypt), was governor of Egypt for more than two years in the early days of Arab leadership. Like Shafi'i's tomb, 'Amr's mausoleum has been restored and reconstructed numerous times over the centuries. As an important Islamic site, it too has attracted the sick, the poor, and the faithful. Many Muslims have chosen to be buried beside this tomb in order to receive the blessings it is thought to possess. In this way, the Cemetery of the Great continued to expand and grow. The Fatimids, who would seize power in Egypt, would add their own distinct contribution to the growing cemetery. Under the Fatimids, the City of the Dead would continue to be an active part of the Muslim community as home not only for the Fatimid dead, but for various groups from society who lived, prayed, worked, and studied among the dead.

THE FATIMIDS 969 A.D.

The Fatimids originated in North Africa early in the tenth century and took control of Egypt in 969 A.D. Their name is taken from Fatima, the Prophet's daughter and the wife of Ali ibn Abu Taleb (Muhammed's cousin and the first convert to Islam). In 969, the Fatimid Caliph al-Mu'izz li-Din Allah sent an army into Egypt under the command of General Gawhar al-Siqilly. General Gawhar and his 100,000 soldiers met little resistance from the residents of of al-Fustat (the Arab name for the Egyptian capital).

Unlike their predecessors, the Fatimids were Shi'i Muslims, claiming descent from the Prophet through his daughter Fatima and hereditary succession through 'Ali, the fourth Caliph (a Caliph is a successor to the Prophet). Although a Sunni Muslim majority, Egyptians generally accepted Shi'i rule during the Fatimid era, as it brought them prosperity and security. After capturing al-Fustat, the Fatimids began construction not far away, on what is now the old city of al-Qahira or Cairo. Al-Qahira became the Fatimid capital in 973 A.D. The name is derived from *Qahir*, the planet Mars, which was in the ascendant when the city was founded. The word is also used to mean "victorious."

Al-Qahira and al-Fustat remained independent cities, and were separated by a massive swamp. Al-Qahira housed the Fatimid Caliph, other members of the Fatimid government, Fatimid soldiers, and servants. The Egyptian middle class resided in al-Fustat. Fortified walls surrounded al-Qahira and protected it from the people of al-Fustat. Egyptians from al-Fustat were forbidden access to al-Qahira after sunset. Likewise, the city of al-Fustat was sealed off from the soldiers of the invading Fatimid army. Nevertheless, the Fatimids continued to use the Cemetery of the Great as their primary burial ground. They extended the cemetery to the northeast, and built much of the mausolea that today constitute the Southern Cemetery. They also built mosques, shrines, and even residences inside the cemeteries and increased the integration of the cemeteries as an active part of the community, not merely a burial ground for the deceased.

Somewhat removed from the main area of the Southern Cemetery and elevated by the Moquattam Hills, is the mosque, and mausoleum of Amr al-Guyushi. A Fatimid wazir (minister), al-Guyushi ruled Egypt for two decades from 1074 to 1094. The mosque dates from 1085 A.D. and commands a magnificent view of Cairo. Although it is not known who is actually buried in the shrine, the building is important as one of the earliest Fatimid monuments. The minaret over the main entrance is thought to be the oldest surviving minaret in Cairo. It is built in typical Fatimid style: a square tower with a smaller square placed on top and covered by a dome.

Also among the most significant still-standing monuments of the Fatimid period are the tombs of Sayyida 'Atika (1122 A.D.) and Muhammad al-Ga'fari (1120 A.D.), members of the family of the Prophet Muhammed. People from around the Muslim world make a pilgrimage to this important burial compound, the largest related group of surviving funerary monuments from the first six centuries of Islam. The tomb chambers are small rooms, with 'Atika's added onto al-Ga'fari's mausoleum. They are deco-

Physical Growth of the Cemeteries

rated simply, but still contain some fine stucco work as well as beautiful *kufic* (the earliest style of Arabic script) inscriptions.

Close to this compound is the tomb of Sayyida Ruqayya. A patron saint of Cairo, Ruqayya was the daughter of 'Ali, the fourth Caliph and the husband of the Prophet's daughter Fatima. Although Ruqayya is actually buried in Damascus, Syria, a shrine was built in Cairo in 1133 A.D. by the wife of the Fatimid Caliph al-Amir. The building is small but handsomely decorated, and it attracts pilgrims from throughout the Muslim world. The shrine's *mihrab* is one of the few remaining in Egypt from the Fatimid era. In the center of the niche is the name of 'Ali surrounded by the name of Muhammed, which is repeated seven times. The tomb is usually adorned with flowers and lace and the smell of perfumes left behind by pilgrims.

Located in the same area of the Cemetery of the Great is the mosque and mausoleum of Sayyida Nafisa, one of the most beloved shrines of the City of the Dead. Given this Muslim saint's reputation for *baraka* and good deeds, many people chose to be buried around the mosque and tomb so they could receive her blessings. The Imam al-Shafi'i lived near Sayyida Nafisa and would visit her to collect traditions of the Prophet. When al-Shafi'i died, his body was brought before her and she recited prayers over it.

Sayyida Nafisa was the granddaughter of al-Hasan (grandson of the Prophet Muhammed). She came to Egypt in the seventh century and lived in a house in the area of what is her present-day mosque. As she felt death approaching, she dug her own grave in this house and prayed there until she died in 824 A.D. The shrine over this tomb has been enlarged and rebuilt many times. In fact, nothing remains of the original buildings. It is believed, however, that this area of the cemetery was built up as people sought to be buried beside this blessed Muslim saint.

The present mosque of Sayyida Nafisa dates to 1897 and is a place of constant activity. Typically, more than one hundred marriages are performed there each week, thus making it one of Cairo's most popular places for wedding ceremonies. Couples wed in Sayyida Nafisa Mosque believing that her blessings will make their marriage strong and long-lasting. The area around this mosque and mausoleum has been an active part of Cairo since the days of Sayyida Nafisa, and it continues to be one of the most urbanized areas of the City of the Dead.

In 1065 A.D., low Nile waters ushered in a seven-year famine, followed by a political crisis that the Fatimids never recovered from. One historian gave this account of Cairo during these dark days, "At last people began to eat each other. Passengers were caught in the streets by hooks let down from windows, drawn up, killed and cooked. Human flesh was sold in public. . . .

The plague came to finish what famine had begun and whole houses were emptied of every living soul in 24 hours."[4] By the middle part of the twelfth century, the Fatimid Dynasty was in irrevocable decline.

THE AYYUBIDS 1171 A.D.

In 1169 A.D., a Kurd from Syria named Salah al-Din Yusuf al-Ayyubi became Prime Minister of Fatimid Egypt and set a course that would bring the dynasty to its end. As a devout Sunni Muslim, Salah al-Din's ambition was to convert Egypt back from Shi'ism. He succeeded, and by 1171 the Fatimid Caliphate was conquered. In 1175, the Abbasid Caliphate in Baghdad named Salah al-Din ruler of Egypt, North Africa, Nubia, Western Arabia, and Syria. Al-Din set out to abolish all traces of Shi'ism, and Egypt once again became the center of the Sunni Muslim Empire. He allowed the palaces of Fatimid rulers to fall into ruin. The remains of one such palace, however, was later uncovered within the City of the Dead's borders. The palace, which bears the inscription of the name of the wife of the first Fatimid Caliph of Egypt, confirms that the ancient Egyptian practice of building residential rooms at or near tomb sites for family visits was a practice adopted by the Fatimids and confirms that the City of the Dead, as an important part of the community, has always been a place for the living as well as the dead. Unlike the palaces, which were largely destroyed or simply neglected, the Fatimid shrines and mausolea remained untouchable, as the saints who are honored and entombed in these shrines are revered by all Muslims, Sunni and Shi'i alike.

Among the monuments of the cemeteries bearing evidence to Ayyubid rule is the tomb of the Abbassid Caliphs. The tomb was constructed in 1242 by a man named Abu Nadla, who served as ambassador to Egypt from the Abbassid Caliphate in Baghdad. The Abbassid Caliphs came to Cairo in 1261, found the tomb Abu Nadla had built, and took it for themselves. The tomb is located directly behind Sayyida Nafisa's Mosque. The Caliphs enlarged the tomb to include ample room for the traditional celebrations for the dead and added accommodations for a tomb keeper. This important mausoleum now contains seventeen tombs, including wooden cenotaphs for Abu Nadla, the sons of the Sultan Baybars, and numerous men and women from the Abbassid family (including the fourth and sixth Caliphs). As in the case with the Mausoleum of the Imam al-Shafi'i, the original *mihrabs* of this complex were not correctly oriented with Mecca. As a result, there are seven *mihrabs* in the tomb.

Physical Growth of the Cemeteries 19

The last Ayyubid building to be built in Cairo was the tomb of Shagar al-Durr (literally, Spray of Pearls). It is a small building, actually a combination of Fatimid and Ayyubid styles. It is made of brick covered with plaster and carved with various decorations. Shagar al-Durr's life was both interesting and unique. The Armenian slave wife of the final male ruler of the Ayyubid Dynasty, Shagar al-Durr was the sole female to rule during Islamic Egypt's lengthy history. Al-Salih Nagm al-Din, Shagar al-Durr's husband, died in 1224 while preparing for battle with the Crusaders. Quick-witted, Shagar al-Durr concealed her husband's death for three months to allow his son, Turan Shah, to return to Egypt from Mesopotamia and inherit the throne.

During this period of concealment, the Mamlukes, an army regiment of Turkish slaves created by Salah al-Din, defeated the Crusaders at the Battle of Mansoura. Rather than gratitude for their defense of the Ayyubid Kingdom, the Mamlukes received only scorn from Turan Shah upon his return. Feeling disgraced, Shagar al-Durr conspired with the Mamluke generals to assassinate her stepson.

After the assassination, Shagar al-Durr proclaimed herself queen and ruled in Turan Shah's name for eighty days. She claimed the right to rule by the fact that she had had a son who survived his father. The phenomenon of female rule proved too incredible for Islamic Egypt of that period as well as for the Abbas sid Caliph in Baghdad. Shagar al-Durr was thus forced into a marriage with Aybak, a Mamluke general (who is said to have been her lover), effectively passing power to a new dynasty.

Shagar al-Durr refused to hand over the throne's treasury to her new husband, however, and their co-rule fell into jeopardy. In defiance, Shagar al-Durr had Aybak murdered as he walked into the palace baths. Her actions were avenged by those loyal to Aybak. She was arrested by the Mamlukes and imprisoned in the Red Tower of the Citadel. There, she was beaten to death and her body is said to have been cast from the tower of the Citadel to dogs waiting below. The body was retrieved and laid to rest in the cemetery in a tomb she had ordered to be constructed during her rule. Shagar al-Durr's life was unprecedented in the history of Egypt and Islam, and with her death ended another era in Cairo's history, an era preserved in the mausolea of the City of the Dead.

THE MAMLUKES 1250 A.D.

The Mamlukes effectively seized power in Egypt in 1250 A.D. The Mamlukes extended the City of the Dead significantly, building some of its most renowned monuments and further integrating this important area of the community by constructing monasteries, residences, and even trade and sporting venues in the cemeteries.

Mamluke rule is typically divided into two periods: the Bahri Mamlukes and the Burgi Mamlukes. Mamlukes were bought as young slaves by older Mamlukes, who raised and educated them. Their training included Arabic, Islam, martial arts, and horsemanship. At puberty, Mamluke boys were manumitted (freed from slavery) and would grow beards. When they reached the age of maturity, they were given land to set up households of their own. They then perpetuated the system of Mamlukes by buying their own young slaves to train. In the words of Count Joseph Arthur:

> The Mamlukes gave the country a complicated, but efficient administration. They had an army whose elements disrupted domestic politics, . . . but which was of proven bravery and was often successful in battle. Egypt was governed by an oligarchy of lost children. . . . In this strange society the freed slave could reach the highest honors of the state, but the free man in the country was bound to the soil in serfdom.[5]

The Bahri Mamlukes ruled prosperously until 1382. They encouraged learning and the arts while they successfully fought off the Crusaders and halted four Mongol invasions. Their successors, the Burgi Mamlukes (of Turco-Circassion and Greek origin), were to rule until their defeat in 1517 at the hands of the Ottomans. However, the Burgi Mamlukes brought a troubled and violent command to the land. Corruption, natural catastrophes, and a loss of military prowess ushered in one of the unhappiest periods in Egypt's history.

Still, the Mamluke era as a whole is characterized by unsurpassed achievement in the arts and architecture. This is evident throughout the City of the Dead. The Mamlukes favored the monumental over the small, as well as painstakingly decorated and varied surfaces. Mosques and mausolea were built to be grand in size, and the arabesque ornamentation of the carved stone domes decorating them are unequaled in the Muslim world. Gobineau described the Mamluke impact:

> In Cairo, the memory of the Mamlukes dominates everything; they accomplished so many things and founded so many solid and beautiful monuments. They alone were able to carve in marble and stone the quantity of arabesques which cover with splendor the buildings of all of Asia. Once these former slaves, the Mamlukes, had their sabres at their sides and the power to

command within their fists, they seemed to be without equal among the Moslem world in the rest of the world.[6]

Under the Mamluke reign, the City of the Dead was extended toward the northeast considerably. By the fourteenth century, the cemetery reached the bridge that leads to modern-day Abbassia, forming what is known as the Northern Cemetery of the City of the Dead. The Northern Cemetery actually began as a hippodrome or a type of circus arena where games were performed. Before this, the area that would become the Northern Cemetery was merely vacant desert outside of the walls of Cairo. Here, the Mamlukes would hold feasts and parties where they would indulge in food and spirits as well as participate in archery contests and horse racing. The first such hippodrome was built by the Sultan An-Nasser Muhammad (1294–1341). Although nothing remains of the Sultan's creation, the mausolea of two of his wives are near to the hippodrome's original site—the tomb of Uzbek Princess Tulbay, which dates to 1363, and that of Qipchaq Princess Tughay, which dates to 1348.

Perhaps no other period of Egyptian history is so well represented in the vast necropolises as that of the Mamlukes. Indeed, Mamluke influence is present from end to end, from the tomb of the Imam al-Lyth at the farthest reaches of the Southern Cemetery to the Mausoleum of the Sultan Inal at the tip of the Northern Cemetery.

The Mamlukes encouraged intellectual pursuits by building schools and Sufi monasteries, many of which lie within the City of the Dead. Many of the monuments of the Northern Cemetery are evidence of the eminence of Sufism during the Mamluke Age. Sufis are Muslim ascetics bound to lead a communal life of prayer and poverty. These monks began to settle in communities in the area that would become the Northern Cemetery. At the time it was an isolated area where they could lead their lives focused on prayer and spirituality without the distractions of the city. Mystical Sufism had existed since the founding of Islam, but by the twelfth century it became a government-supported institution in Egypt. Complexes were built in the cemetery honoring Sufi saints. The complexes would contain the saint's mausoleum, mosques, *khanqahs* (gathering places for prayer and learning), and living quarters for resident Sufis as well as for the father of the Sufi order, to be used during his visits. The importance of such institutions during this time is evidenced by the fact that Mamluke Sultans frequently built their own living quarters and mausolea inside these Sufi complexes. These complexes, however, were expensive to maintain, and with the fall of the Mamlukes, many of them fell into a state of disrepair. Cairo historian

Dorothea Russell observed that, "It is not surprising that they were allowed to fall into ruin in a later age that knew not the great men who created them."[7] Fortunately, more recent times have brought many of the complexes some much needed restoration.

One of the major Mamluke complexes in the Northern Cemetery is that of the Sultan Barquq. The first of the Burgi Mamlukes, Sultan Barquq ruled from 1382–99. His mortuary complex was built over the course of eleven years by his son, who honored his request to be buried next to the tombs of revered Sufi sheikhs. The complex is built in massive Mamluke-style architecture and contains twin domes, twin minarets, as well as a pair of *sabil-kuttabs* (public drinking fountains and Quaranic schools for boys). At the structure's entrance there is a carved piece from a Pharaonic monument, which is used as a doorstep. The idea behind its use is to crush the pagan religion in a literal and figurative sense.

After a lengthy hall, the complex opens up into a square sanctuary, each side measuring 240 feet. The open court is square in shape, and it is bordered on all sides by arcades and chambers. The structure is four stories high, with cells for Sufi dervishes located off the courtyard. The tomb-chambers occupy the back corners and are topped by two of the earliest stone domes in Cairo. The chambers are separated from the sanctuary by beautiful *mashrabiyya* (wooden lattice with lace grill work) screens. Located in the arcade between the tomb-chambers is the *minbar* (pulpit), which is made of ivory inlaid in an arabesque pattern. The pulpit, donated by the Sultan Qaytbay in 1483, is unusual for the time in that the decoration is carved in stone rather than wood.

The madrasa of Sultan Barquq's complex contained areas for each of the four rites of Islam to be taught. The twin minarets rise high above the structure, their first half in rectangular form and the top half circular. The two tombs contain the remains of Barquq and his sons, Farag and Abd al'Aziz, in one chamber, and the remains of two of Farag's daughters, Shiriz and Shakra, in the other. The twin chambers are lit by a group of stained glass windows framed with stucco. The fact that men and women are buried in separate chambers demonstrates that the sexes were kept apart even in death, a custom still in practice today.

The Barquq complex was also an attempt to urbanize an area that was largely desert at the time it was built. This allowed the complex to be designed without size restraints. Included in the design for the complex were not only living quarters, but baths, bakeries, markets, grain mills, and rooms for visitors, all of which were to be connected by a series of alleys and streets. The Sultan, however, did not live to see the completion of of the complex.

Not far to the south of Barquq's complex is that of the Sultan al-Ashraf Barsbay. Like Barquq's, Barsbay's complex consists of a mausoleum, a madrasa, and two sabils. The madrasa-mosque is very elegant, containing two *liwans* (vaulted spaces) with a path down the center separated by a pair of arcades. The madrasa contained living quarters for the Sultan and his Sufi sheikh, with attached quarters for Sufi disciples. The architecture and interior decoration is very impressive. The complex is known for its marble mosaic pavements as well as for the height and ornamentation of the main dome of the mausoleum. The interlacing pattern carved on the outside of the dome is a star motif and was the first of its kind. Barsbay ruled from 1422 to 1438, and his mortuary complex was constructed in 1430. He is best known for his conquest of Cyprus.

To the north of Barquq's complex is a compound that is actually two complexes joined together, that of the Sultan Inal and that of the Amir Qurqumas. Sultan Inal's complex is the earlier structure, dating to 1451–56. Its physical composition reflects the life of the man whose name it bears. Inal lived a long life in which he ascended to progressive levels of power and authority. Separate sections of his complex mark each era of his ascension to power. The mausoleum was built when he was Amir. In 1451, when he became Sultan, the khanqh, madrasa-mosque, a sabil, and a *zawiya* (a residence for Muslim Sufis centered around a sheikh) were added. As a result, the complex has an odd appearance. The dome, built early in the construction, sits quite low in proportion to the rest of the structure.

Attached to Sultan Inal's complex is that of the Amir Qurqumas al-Kabir, which was built in the early sixteenth century. Qurqumas, Grand Amir and Commander-in-Chief of the Army, built this mausoleum before his death in 1510. In addition to the mausoleum, the complex contained numerous buildings including a *rab'* (apartment building), which was used to accommodate travelers and to provide monetary support for the complex's operating costs. It also contained a madrasa-mosque, residential quarters, a sabil-kuttab, as well as kitchens, storerooms, stables, waterwheels, and an ablution court.

During the British occupation of Egypt, the structure was used as a storeroom for gunpowder. In more modern times, the two complexes have been undergoing extensive restoration by the Polish-Egyptian Group for Restoration of Islamic Monuments.

The complex of the Amir Qurqumas is similar in arrangement to the neighboring complex of the Sultan Qaytbay, but lacks the ornamentation and genius for which Qaytbay's mausoleum is renowned. Indeed, the complex of the Sultan al-Ashraf Qaytbay is the most celebrated mausoleum of the Northern Cemetery. It is here that Mamluke architecture and art reached their zenith and the height of this achievement can be viewed.

Qaytbay began his career as one of Barsbay's Mamlukes, bought for fifty dinars. Known for his combat skills, virility, and management abilities, he rose through the ranks of the Mamlukes to become Commander-in-Chief of the Army and, ultimately, Sultan. Under his rule, the Muslim Empire witnessed a great period of building and restoration. His own complex dates from 1472–74, and once formed a large, enclosed compound consisting of nine buildings. Included in the original design were traveler's lodgings, which were rented to defray the cost of maintenance, a burial ground for members of the Sultan's family, drinking troughs for animals, as well as waterwheels that supplied the complex. The tomb chamber also contains fossilized footprints said to belong to the Prophet Muhammed. In its early years the complex was surrounded by desert and was a popular stop on the trade routes between Egypt, the Red Sea, and Syria.

The main structure of Qaytbay's complex (which appears on the Egyptian one pound note) consists of a madrasa-mosque, tomb chambers, and a courtyard. Attached to the mausoleum is a hall containing the tombs of the Sultan's four wives. The outside of the building is made of red and white striped masonry (*ablaq*), and on the inside, ornate decoration abounds. Floors, doors, walls, windows, and ceilings are flowered with geometric and arabesque designs, as well as with elegant Islamic calligraphy. The individual designs combine to form a stunning vision.

From the roof, the dome and minaret can be examined, and the considerable size of the complex can be appreciated. The dome is considered to be the finest in all of Cairo. It has two intricately carved designs: a raised straight-lined star pattern and a recessed lacework of floral arabesques. This ornate detail is painstakingly reproduced on the three-tiered, 130-foot high minaret. The minaret rises into the sky above the City of the Dead and provides a panoramic view of the Northern Cemetery.

From atop Qaytbay's minaret, the Bab al-Wazir Cemetery, across Salah Salem Highway, can be seen. Here, other important Mamluke monuments are found. These include the mausoleum of Mangak al-Yusufi, former viceroy of Egypt and commander-in-chief of the army. Yusufi built his mausoleum in 1349 and died in 1375. The two-story complex included the mosque, a khanqah, a free-standing minaret, and a covered courtyard. In the back of the khanqah is a tunnel that is rumored to lead to the Citadel of Muhammad 'Ali.

Physical Growth of the Cemeteries

A view of the Northern Cemetery from on top of the Qaytbay Mosque.

The Mausoleum of Yunus al-Dawadar, also in the Bab al-Wazir Cemetery, is a short walk from Yusufi's complex. This tomb is the earliest monument of the Burgi Mamlukes dating to 1382. Yunus al-Dawadar was the royal messenger to the Sultan Barquq. Appropriately, his name means Jonah the inkbottle holder. The mausolea, in bad need of restoration, has an impressive minaret that is topped by a ribbed dome. Yunus, however, was never buried in the structure. He was killed in Syria and it is unclear where his body was buried.

THE OTTOMANS 1517 A.D.

The City of the Dead continued to be the city's main burial ground and an important part of the community after the Ottoman conquest of Egypt. There are numerous impressive monuments from the post-Mamluke era. One of the most striking is the khanqh and tomb of Shahin al-Kalawati, which dramatically sits atop an outcropping of the Moquattam Hills, its minaret silhouetted against the sky and the hill's limestone slopes. Little is known of this structure that was built in 1538 A.D. by members of the

Kalawati order of Islamic mystics in Iran. The mausoleum's location makes it almost impossible to reach, a feat that involves a considerable climb. The effort, however, is rewarded by a stunning view of the Southern Cemetery with the buildings of downtown Cairo forming a distant backdrop. On a clear day, the pyramids are visible lurking in the desert on the opposite side of the city.

Today, the history of Egypt and the growth of Islam can be traced through the monuments seen atop this tomb. Family tombs from the Ottomans, who seized control of Egypt from the Mamlukes in 1517 A.D., are also visible, as well as many restored shrines in the Turkish style. One can visit the tomb of the family of Muhammad 'Ali, the founder of modern Egypt. The tomb, called Howsh al-Basha, was built in 1820 and is located behind the tomb of the Imam al-Shafi'i. This complex is made of a shrine with five domes and a large courtyard. From the outside, this once-grand structure looks like a ruin. The inside, however, is well maintained by the family and there is a tomb-keeper to escort visitors through the parade of cenotaphs and gravestones. Those buried here include three sons of Muhammad 'Ali by his first wife along with their wives and children. Numerous servants and counselors of the family are also buried in the compound in addition to a number of Mamlukes who were purchased by Muhammad 'Ali to act as bodyguards and servants. Muhammad 'Ali, however, is not buried here. Rather, his remains lie in his mosque in the Citadel.

The cenotaphs and gravestones of Howsh al-Basha are decorated in a baroque Ottoman style, carved with colorful garlands and floral designs. The sex and official grade of the dead is portrayed by stela atop the cenotaphs and gravestones, which are carved with the appropriate head coverings: fezzes, turbans, coronets, and tresses. The effect is striking as the cenotaphs become personified, and walking among them one feels as if they are in the presence of true royalty.

SOCIAL CHANGE IN THE CEMETERIES

The brief French occupation of 1798–1801 appears to have made one major contribution to the City of the Dead: a change in the Egyptian attitude toward cemeteries. The historic belief in Egypt that cemeteries are an active part of the community and not exclusively for the dead dates back to ancient times. Islam adapted to this aspect of Egyptian tradition. The French appear, however, to have brought a more Western view of cemeteries to Egypt. The presence of people living and carrying out other activities in the cemeteries became unacceptable to urbanized Egyptians aspiring to be like their

European counterparts. The cemetery began to be seen as a place for only the dead. The only acceptable reason to visit the cemetery was for funerals, visitation of the deceased on birthdays and religious holidays, and prayer. People living in or carrying out other activities in the cemeteries were seen as being removed from mainstream society and uncultured. This perspective was reinforced during the subsequent British presence in Egypt. Although the City of the Dead continued to provide housing for numerous Cairenes, and a refuge for the sick and poor, as well as a retreat for religious pilgrims, such activities were increasingly ignored, condemned, and shamed by the majority of Cairene society.

At the start of the twentieth century, the City of the Dead began to grow in importance once again. The World Wars aggravated Cairo's ability to provide housing for its increasing numbers. The City of the Dead became an increasingly popular shelter for the homeless. Janet Abu-Lughod describes the scene: "The stream of migrants that had begun to head for Cairo during the early war years increased to flood proportions during the last years of the war and the several years of economic prosperity that ensued."[8] She continues, "Residential construction virtually ceased at the very time when the city was attracting so many new residents. Thus, by 1947, the city's facilities were badly strained. Older quarters that had been fully built up and overcrowded even during the preceding decades became even more densely packed. . . . Close to 50,000 persons were living in the cemetery zones alone."[9]

The rise of the housing crisis in the twentieth century has made it impossible to ignore the role of the City of the Dead in providing infrastructure for more than Cairo's dead as the number of people living in the cemeteries has swelled. The 50,000 residents of the City of the Dead in 1947 had risen to 80,000–90,000 in 1960 and to greater than 100,000 in 1970.[10] Today, the population estimate stands at greater than 500,000. This spectacle of contemporary Egypt's contribution to the cemeteries is shocking. The cemeteries of the City of the Dead have come to provide informal housing for hundreds of thousands of Egypt's indigent. In most cases, they have settled in the cemeteries not because they believe that the City of the Dead should be an active and dynamic part of the community. They have settled there out of necessity as Cairo has been unable to provide adequate and affordable housing for hundreds of thousands of its residents. By looking back at the long tradition in Egypt of life among the dead, these people who have settled among the tombs have found a creative, albeit undesirable, answer for their plight.

STORIES

> When we first arrived [in the City of the Dead] I was shocked to see the place where we would live. There was so much dirt and dust, and garbage was piled everywhere . . . and the noise! Everything was brown. I immediately missed the green of the countryside.
> —Zekia Imbabi
> Resident of the Northern Cemetery

Women in the City of the Dead are faced with the daily challenges of poor women throughout the Third World who are trying to eke out an existence for themselves and their families on the edges of subsistence. They must find time and means to put food on the table, make their meager form of shelter into a home, raise their children, and fulfill their husbands' needs. Little time is left for themselves. Their lives are devoted to others. Often, these challenges require great sacrifice and seem insurmountable in the face of a patrimonial society and a modest code of conduct required of women. For these women, life is a balancing act. So often, however, they prove themselves able to endure again and again in the face of great odds.

ZEINAB ALI
Life's Wisdom

Zeinab Ali, now an elderly woman whose appearance reflects the sixty plus years of change and austerity she has witnessed in her lifetime, was forced to become an adult early in life. As a young teenager in a poor Cairo community, she was suddenly thrust into womanhood, wifehood, and motherhood, and taken away from her familiar environment, family, and roots and brought into the world of the City of the Dead.

Zeinab can look back on her life and recall events with vivid detail and emotion. Although she has never had it easy, she doesn't view her situation with self-pity. Rather, she prefers to talk of what she has gained in life—wisdom.

I attended school for only one year as it was customary at that time among traditional families to keep girls uneducated. I don't look back on my lack of education with sorrow or regret, however. 'Life' has been my education and that is the best education that you can get! There are so many people who have spent years and years in schools and universities and yet they

Physical Growth of the Cemeteries

know so little about how to live or how to survive in life. I don't care about the number of years a person has spent studying in school. It's not important. It doesn't impress me. What they studied is equally as unimportant. Rather, what you learn from life is what really matters. People need to observe the community and the world around them and learn from that. They can't just stick their noses into books! They have to take care to understand life. This is the way in which they can acquire the wisdom which they will need to take with them to the next life, the life after death.

Zeinab's life changed radically at the age of fourteen when she married and moved from the poor Cairo area of Sayyida Aisha to live with her new husband in the cemetery nearby. There she would spend the rest of her life and she remains there today, a half-century later.

You are probably surprised that I got married when I was fourteen. That was normal in those days and I don't regret it at all. Of course, it wasn't my decision. My parents simply informed me one day that I was to become engaged and that when the time came for the actual marriage, I would leave them and become part of a new family. Of course I was scared but I was also excited. After all, getting married was the dream and goal of all young girls as soon as they were able to have dreams and goals. I was certainly well prepared for marriage at that time. Girls were taught how to be wives and mothers from a very early age. I was either helping with or had completely taken over all of my mother's household duties by the time that I was twelve. I had proven that I was ready to take on the responsibilities of marriage and motherhood. That was the only thing that was important in those days—that the girls be well prepared to carry out their primary functions in life. It wasn't like today where girls are sent to school to learn about things which really don't concern them and which distract from their true duties.

The decision for my new husband and me to move to the cemetery was both economic and practical. We were a young, newly married couple without any savings. The area provided inexpensive housing. It was also practical because my husband was going to work as a tombkeeper and undertaker. Talk about an ideal place for him to live! At first, the idea of living in the cemetery frightened me. I was afraid of the jiin which might live there. I knew that my new husband would protect me from them but what would happen during the long hours when he was away from our room? Over time, however, I got used to being home along with the jiin. Maybe they are my friends now! Of course, when we moved here we were two of only a handful of people who had taken up permanent residence in this part of the cemetery. As you can see, over the years more and more people have come to live here. They are good people and have formed a nice community. I don't feel alone now like I did in the old days, except when I think about my late husband and my children.

Zeinab's husband died over twenty years ago but she still continues to live in their single room in the Cemetery of the Great not far from Sayyida Nafisa Mosque. Every morning she gets up to carry out her household duties as well as those of her late husband.

I get up early every morning. I've never slept late one day in my whole life. I wash my face, pray, and eat something small for breakfast—bread and cheese or anything that I may happen to have. I quickly do chores around my room and any washing that needs to be done.

When this is taken care of, she heads out across the dusty path which runs between the labyrinth of tombs. Here, she enters the tomb of Sidi Gohara.

Perhaps this is my favorite place on earth. Of course I haven't seen too many places! I think that it would still be my favorite place though. Of course I would like to make the pilgrimage to the holy city to visit the ka'aba where Muhammed did his great deeds and taught God's words. Still, I am happy to be blessed as the caretaker for one of God's most divine followers.

Zeinab enters the tombs, sweeps the floor of the chamber, and splashes water outside the tomb's door to prevent dust from filling the air. When this is done, she sits down on the steps of the tomb in the shade of the roof's overhang. She is proud to recite the history of the tomb she tends.

Sidi Gohara was Sayyida Nafisa's servant hundreds of years ago. Before the blessed Sayyida Nafisa died, she told all of her followers that anyone who would come to visit her and pay their respects after she had passed away should first go and visit Sidi Gohara's tomb. Her words have been taken to heart by many of the pilgrims who have come to the cemetery to pay homage to the two ladies as both tombs continue to be places of visitation by the faithful.

After completing her cleaning, Zeinab simply rests her aged body on the steps of the tomb. She sits in the shade with her legs and bare feet dangling to one side. It is here that she will spend the major part of her day waiting to greet any visitors who come to pay their respects to the dead. She waits for the conversation they will bring, hoping for company with whom to pass the hours.

Physical Growth of the Cemeteries

Zeinab talks with pride about her family to anyone willing to listen:

I am mother to one son and one daughter. I felt that my life was complete as a woman when I gave my husband our son. Children are the greatest source of a mother's pride. I guess that I had wanted more children but it was difficult enough with four people living in one room!

Both of my children are happily married with large families. Mohamed, my son, went to the university and studied agriculture. This was his father's idea. You know what my opinion of education is. Still, I'm proud of him for succeeding at it. We had to make many sacrifices so that he was able to go. When he graduated he was given a low-paying government job, which had nothing to do with what he had studied. I told you that education was unimportant! Look what it got him after all of those sacrifices! When his father died, Mohamed fulfilled his duties as the only son by stepping into his father's shoes and taking over his father's responsibilities. He has found that working as a tombkeeper and undertaker is actually more profitable than his ridiculous government job. He still works at his inherited profession to this day, but he lives with his wife and three daughters (they are still hoping to have a son, god willing) in the cemetery near Sayyida Aisha not very far away. My room would have been too small for him to stay here after he was married. He wanted me to live with him and his family, but I didn't want to leave this place which I have called home for so many years. I didn't want to be a burden on them, and I have my responsibilities to God and to Sidi Gohara. Still, he is close enough so that he comes and visits often and leaves me well provided for. He's been a good son.

Zeinab claims that, in spite of her relatively solitary and meager life, she is happy.

I enjoy the quiet of the cemetery except, of course, when the silence is broken by the crying of a passing funeral and the air is filled with pain. Also, the air is fairly clean here. It is not like I hear it is in the center of Cairo. I suppose that quiet and fresh air are two things which are very hard to find much of in a city like Cairo, but I enjoy them here. I also enjoy the company of my neighbors. Our difficult lives have brought us closer together, and we help each other when we are in need. People who live in the upper-class areas of Cairo waste too much time worrying about themselves. The people who live beside me, however, are normal, friendly, and respectable people. The air among us here is not that which is typical of a big city. Rather, it is more like a small village where everyone knows each other and cares about one another.

Zeinab boasts about the many services that she has in her one-room tomb-home as compared to others living around her; services they can only dream about:

Because of the closeness of my home to the Sayyida Nafisa Mosque and the more urbanized area nearby, I have had running water and electricity for years. Also, my late husband got a telephone wire run to our room. Thirty years ago it wasn't expensive like it is today. Of course, it was necessary for my husband to have a telephone because of his work. In this way, when someone died and needed to be buried in the area of the cemetery which was under my husband's jurisdiction, he could be contacted immediately and would have time to make the proper arrangement for the burial. I still enjoy the use of the telephone after all these years, but calls are fewer and farther between and costs keep rising and rising. I know that I am fortunate to have it though because most people walk to the coffee house, which borders one side of Sayyida Nafisa Mosque, to use the community telephone. I don't know if my feeble legs would take me that far any more!

The expense of the telephone is only one of Zeinab's many complaints about today's costs of living.

Everything costs so much money. Even living here in the cemetery and avoiding most of the so-called modern world, it is difficult to make ends meet. Ten pounds every month for water, forty-eight pounds every six months for the telephone, money for food, money for electricity. . . . It is a large list of expenses. Where can I get the money? Thank God that I have my son, and I can rely on him to make sure that all is well. God bless him. Also, God bless the generous people who come to visit Sidi Gohara and award me for my hard work and watchful eye.

My life may not be interesting to most people, but it is satisfying to me and I thank God for everything that He has given to me over all of these years. I will continue to live and I will die in this cemetery. I will continue to perform my daily routine until God no longer needs me to. Life has been my teacher and I have been a good and faithful student, although it has never been easy.

During the long hours in which she sits alone in the shade of Gohara's tomb, she often finds herself reflecting on life's lessons. She is willing to offer advice to anyone who seeks it at all, especially the young:

I've lived a long and healthy life and I've spent a lot of time thinking about life in general. I warn the young today not to get caught up in the material and elitist world. Young people are so different today, especially the girls. They have forgotten their proper roles and have ignored the lessons of their ancestors. They spend years studying outrageous school lessons and then insist on working along side of the men in offices and shops. They leave their kids uncared for and stay outside of the home late into the night. I feel bad for the young men. It is better if they don't get married at all. Today with marriage comes paying for a flat, paying for a doorman, paying for nice clothes, paying to educate children . . . paying, paying, paying. Everything revolves around money. These things are not necessary! It is better if you live simply, and if you simply live alone!

ZEKIA IMBABI
Village without Fields

Zekia Imbabi lives in a three-story building built over a tomb in the Northern Cemetery. From her window she can look out over the dusty main street to the courtyard of the mausoleum of the Sultan Barsbay. Her home, however, among the tombs of the Mamluke rulers and thousands of others like herself, is far from her roots.

I grew up in a village in the Fayyum area [some 55 miles south-west of Cairo in Middle Egypt]. *It was a farming community and I can remember playing in the beautiful green fields as a small girl. The color green is still so strong in my mind. There is nothing like it here in Cairo.*

One summer day in particular stands out in her mind as if it were one week or even one day ago.

I was out in the fields. I don't know if I was doing more working or playing. Anyway, as usual I had to do my share of the family chores: cooking and cleaning, working in the fields, and cutting clover to feed the water buffalo and the donkeys. This day started out as a normal day. When I returned home from the fields, however, I found my mother eagerly and excitedly waiting for me. I couldn't imagine what had made her so happy, but she quickly told me. My cousin had visited my family home that afternoon. He had asked a lot of questions about me and finally had announced that he wished to marry me! I was devastated, afraid, and confused all at the same time. I could think of nothing to say in response to what I had been told. Instead of talking, I responded with tears. I knew that my primary responsibility was to get married and have sons. My mother had been teaching me how to run a household for as long as I could remember. Still, I never expected it to come so soon! I knew that I was supposed to be as excited and as pleased as my mother was, but all I could do was cry. I don't really know why. I just had the strangest feeling inside. I thought that it was a tragedy.

In spite of her crying, she became engaged at the age of nine.

My engagement lasted three years, and during that time I learned to accept my situation. Here in Egypt it is good for a girl to get married young before she has a chance to get into trouble and become spoiled. Many of my girlfriends in the village also became engaged, and we spent most of our time together sharing our fears and concerns about what married life would bring us. I secretly wondered if I was ready to take on such responsibilities. What if I didn't please my husband? What if he treated me badly? What if I couldn't give him a son? What if he divorced me or, even worse, took another wife? There were so many questions and uncertainties. I did become n.ore comfortable, however, as I began to know my husband-to-be in the brief times that he would come to sit with my family. In any case, I had to accept my destiny and do my best. After all, I really didn't have a choice!

At the age of twelve, Zekia became a child-bride and moved to live with her new husband's family in Beni Suef, a town in Middle Egypt some 80 miles south of Cairo.

I found myself in a strange place with a family which was equally as strange to me and with many responsibilities I had to carry out well enough to please all of my new relatives. As a new bride, I knew that even the smallest tasks I did would be scrutinized to the very last detail. At first, I found my new environment to be hostile. I was surrounded by people, but I felt alone. My new family claimed me as a daughter, sister, and wife, but I felt more like a servant. I remember the nights I spent crying and longing to return to my real family and the familiar surroundings of my home village. At times, however, I was angry with them and felt as if they had betrayed me by giving me up. I longed for them and at the same time I blamed them for my unhappiness. Now, when I look back at those days, I realize that I was just a scared child who was resisting growing up. In fact, my husband was a good man and I was not treated any differently from any other newly married girl.

My new relatives were also farmers like the family I had left. As a farmer's wife, I was expected to tend to the house, work in the fields, and (of course) to have and care for children. I soon had a daughter to care for and to love even though I was barely a young woman myself. It was soon after the birth of my daughter that what may be called the second tragedy of my life

Physical Growth of the Cemeteries 35

occurred. My husband and partner in my young marriage (God bless him) suddenly fell ill and died. The doctors said that he was possessed by an evil spirit. I was left widowed with a small child in a household that I didn't feel was my own. It was an unenviable position to be in! I prayed to God and asked Him what I had done which was so horrible that I deserved this punishment. Was it because I hadn't accepted my marriage in the first place?

It was a very difficult time in my life. Of course, it would not be very well if I stayed living with my husband's family as a widow. Likewise, it would not be well if I returned with my baby to my family in Fayyum. Fortunately (thank God), as was customary in traditional Egypt, one of my husband's cousins came forth and married me in order to relieve me and my child of our desperate situation.

It was through this marriage that Zekia would come to be among the residents of the City of the Dead.

With the sudden and unexpected addition of a wife and a daughter who were dependent on him for support, my new husband decided to move our young family to the city in search of money and opportunity. He had visited the city and had heard of the cemetery as an inexpensive starting point for newcomers to Cairo, and he knew others from the countryside who had settled there before us. I was filled with fear and hope, and I prayed to God that my husband's decision would bring us safety and happiness. I think, however, that I was almost as scared of going to the city as I was of getting married a few years before. I was especially scared for my baby and the harm that living in the cemetery might bring to her, particularly after the death of her father by evil spirits.

My husband and I made a home here, in the Northern Cemetery. When we first arrived I was shocked to see that this was the place where we would live. There was so much dirt and dust, and garbage was piled everywhere . . . and the noise! Everything was brown. I immediately missed the green of the countryside. Here, there were no plants to be found. To me there was no life here at all. It was ugly and awful. I hated it from the first moment that I saw it. On top of all of this, there were dead people sleeping under my feet!

We paid the owner of the tomb where we would live twenty-five piasters every month. I guess that I never would have imagined that fifty years later I would still be in the same place. My husband had always intended for us to move out of the cemetery and live in a real home.

As she remained stationary, however, many changes were taking place around her.

Every year, more and more people have come to live in the cemetery. It has grown at a tremendous pace as people move in but are seldom able to leave. This area is getting to be quite crowded but I am sure that it will get worse before it gets any better.

With the people have come electricity, running water, and telephones in some areas. They have also, however, brought with them pollution, garbage, and additional poverty. I think that the bad has outweighed the good.

My second husband managed to find work unloading trucks and was able to provide an acceptable life for our family. I gave him a son and raised both of my children to become good young adults. Although my husband tried his best (God bless him), he was never able to achieve his goal of having us move out of the cemetery before he died. Once again, I found myself alone in a strange world. Of course this time I had the company of my children who would support me in my old age, and I myself had matured with the experience life had brought.

Today Zekia can be seen sitting on a rock in front of the tomb she has learned to call home. She is one of the neighborhood door-sitters who is constantly watching the actions of everybody outside to see who is passing by, who is visiting who, and who has some new possession. Second only to her household chores, gossiping is her most important activity. She is always searching for the news.

She now lives in one of the original two rooms she had occupied with her late husband and children. Her son and his family have taken over the adjoining room. Her son works in Cairo's informal transportation system and has managed to save up enough money to buy an old microbus, which he uses to transport passengers. His teenage son, Mohamed, dropped out of school in his last year of preparatory and began working as an assistant to a mechanic. Still, he will confess that his real desire is to learn to speak English.

Upstairs from Zekia are two rooms for the owner of the tomb-house and his family. Ahmed, who inherited ownership upon the death of his father (who is buried in the tomb), lives with his sister, her husband and children. A telephone operator in Cairo, Ahmed also buys, cleans, and re-sells rice for extra income. He can usually be found sitting in the afternoons with Zekia outside of the tomb beside bags of rice piled on red soda cartons. Behind his young but feeble form (he has cerebral palsy) the outer walls of the tomb are covered with paintings of airplanes and the sea, gaily portraying his sister's journey to Saudi Arabia to perform the Muslim pilgrimage or *hajj*.

Zekia has never been to Saudi Arabia but her pilgrimage was made long ago: the common trek of the migrant to the unknown city, in search of the things upon which hopes and dreams are built. Although her surroundings have changed as more and more people have settled in the cemetery, her values, traditions, and culture have largely remained the same. Over time, her fear of the City of the Dead has subsided. She accepted and made the cemetery her home and has even grown fond of the area and its people.

This area is not like the city. We all know each other here. If a stranger or someone who doesn't belong comes here, we know it. We are all from the country and this cemetery has become a village without fields.

Sometimes Zekia is able to travel back to Middle Egypt and visit her relatives there. Always, however, she returns to the City of the Dead. For her, this place has become her home. She has grown comfortable living among the tombs and among the other poor like herself. She says about the cemetery:

I hope that I die here. I wouldn't want to die any place else.

Fatima Ali
The Black Sheep

I have to be careful because there are thieves around here and everyone wants to steal my black sheep. I'm surprised it isn't dead from the evil eye. There are so many jealous people.

Fatima Ali rattles off these words as she gazes fondly at a shaved black sheep tied to a post in front of her tomb-dwelling. The sheep, which cost more than 200 Egyptian pounds (LE), is to help her family celebrate the *Eid El Kabir* (Big Feast) and, according to her, is the envy of the area.

I don't talk to most people I don't know. I'm afraid that they'll try and take something from me. I don't have a lot, but they will take whatever they can get their hands on. One time, some nice people (so I thought at the time) stopped by and started chatting with me in front of the house. We spent half of the afternoon talking about this and that as if we were old friends or relatives. Then, one of them asked me for a glass of water. When I went inside to fetch it, one of them snuck in behind me and stole my radio! Really! I haven't trusted anyone since then.

The cemetery wasn't always so dangerous. I used to trust people years ago. Of course that was before it got so crowded. Everyone used to know everyone else, and we were more like one big extended family. Nowadays, I don't know half of the people who walk by my door. More and more people keep coming here and they bring more and more problems with them.

I was born in the cemetery, and I've lived here all of my life. That wasn't true for my parents though. They migrated here from a village in Upper Egypt. Why? I don't know. I guess so many people kept telling them how wonderful the city was they decided to take a chance. Of course it wasn't true. I know that my mother at least was always unhappy here and always used to tell me about her home in Upper Egypt. I've never been there, but I've heard the stories of the clean air, the green fields, and the good people. I think that being away from this killed her. She died very young. I believe it was from unhappiness. I always wanted to go to Upper Egypt and see what it is like for myself, but I've never been able to. I don't think that there is much hope now. I'm too old!

Fatima's sixty-plus years show on her worn face. She has had a full life of responsibilities, having had to care for her family at a very young age after her mother's death. She has witnessed changing times in Egypt and the cemetery from the perspective of her tomb-home on the main road of the Northern Cemetery across from the complex of the Sultan Baybars. The one-story structure, which is built over a tomb, is decorated with faded pictures portraying Fatima's husband's holy pilgrimage to Saudi Arabia. It is ironic to see her sitting in front of pictures of an airplane buzzing by her head and a ship sailing past her knee, knowing that she probably has never ventured far beyond the streets surrounding her home. Here she sits day after day, cleaning rice or shelling peas and all the while keeping a watchful eye over the activities taking place in the street. She waits for her husband to return from work.

We are poor but I thank God for what we do have. I don't complain much because it doesn't do any good. Of course, this is the only life I have ever known. Maybe I would complain more if I knew exactly what I am missing. My husband does. For all I know, all of the world could live like this. My husband, however, sees the world outside of the cemetery. He'll come home and talk about how bad things are here. I listen to him politely, but I really don't want to know. We are not starving. We have a roof over our heads. We have our health (Although I worry about that constantly. What would happen if my husband got seriously ill?). What else can I ask for? Anyway, our suffering in this life will make the next life even sweeter.

My husband has always had a job (thank God). There are many people in this area who don't work at all. When my parents came here many years ago, when it wasn't crowded like it is today, they were able to save up enough money for my father to open up a small shop nearby for building materials. That is what my husband does now. He worked with my father from the day that we were married. He became the son my father had never had. The shop was left for him to run when my father died because I have no brothers and my uncles are either dead or live in the countryside far away.

My husband is a good man. He treats me well (thank God), and we've had a long life together in which we have been relatively happy. There was only one period of my life when I wasn't happy. That was when my only son died. That was the most devastating time of my life. It is the most difficult thing for a mother to go through. A child should not die before his mother. It was God's will, however, and I had to accept that.

My son was sent away to fight in the 1973 War against Israel in the Sinai. We were so nervous and upset when he left. He was our only son and he was so young! He was still a boy. We were proud, however, that he would be defending our country, Egypt. When we didn't hear from him for a long time we began to worry more than usual. Of course communication was difficult during this time. Still, I began to feel inside that something was terribly wrong. Even after the fighting had ended, we heard nothing from our son. Finally, it was reported to us that he was missing, unaccounted for. What did that mean? Was he dead or alive? Well, they were burying the bodies of the unknown soldiers at the War Cemetery, a five minutes walk from here. One of the men who was helping in this task and who lives in the area recognized one of the corpses as my son. They were going to bury my boy as an unknown soldier! My only baby was dead! My husband went to identify the body. It was true. It was him, my only son, the pride and joy of my life. We were devastated. I didn't think I would make it through this time. What did he do? I blamed the army. I blamed the Israelis. I blamed God. I blamed myself. Finally, I accepted our fate. We brought the body of my son here and buried it in our home where I can always be beside him until I can join him. That will be a truly wonderful day.

2

THE MODERN ERA: INFORMAL HOUSING IN THE CITY OF THE DEAD

> Those who leave their homes should bear misery as well as insults.
> —Arab Proverb

The mausolea of the City of the Dead represent a long and glorious history set in the cradle of civilization. The modern face of the cemeteries, however, represents with the same accuracy the problems and challenges Egypt and its people face today. Population has swelled in this country, where 96 percent of the land is desert; the urban-rural gap has widened so that the two communities are in many cases two different worlds; migrants from the countryside have swarmed to the metropolis in alarming numbers; and Cairo has become the leading city of Egypt, absorbing a population far beyond its means and resources. These pressures have created the modern phenomenon of the City of the Dead, a refuge for the urban poor, the indigent, and the disenfranchised of society.

INFORMAL HOUSING

In Cairo, a person who works at a secure, mid-level occupation is fortunate in comparison to his countrymen among the ranks of the unemployed and subemployed. Even so, such a job does not always guarantee a person such necessities of life as adequate housing.

Enormous numbers of people in Egypt cannot afford decent housing. Surprisingly, however, there is no housing shortage per se. In fact, Cairo is filled with buildings that are half-empty. These vacancies exist for three basic reasons: the apartments are being held for future occupancy by relatives of the owners, usually for children when they get married; the apartments are in luxury buildings that are unaffordable for the vast majority of Egyptians; or the apartments are being withheld from sale by their owners in anticipation of a better housing market.

In addition to a surplus of vacant units in established buildings, new buildings are continually under construction. The question of housing is not so much of availability as it is of affordability. An Abt Associates study commissioned by the United States Agency for International Development (USAID) concluded that "there are indeed major housing needs among Egyptians but these are more related to specific features of housing cost than the ability of households to find shelter."[11]

The final price of most apartments in Cairo are well beyond the capacity of the average (and, in many cases, above-average) Egyptian's income. A modest new apartment in the Cairo suburb of Nasr City, for example, may cost 40,000 Egyptian pounds (LE), or approximately $12,000, without any furnishings, plumbing, or paint. Such amenities are likely to double the price tag. For the average Egyptian who earns a monthly salary of between LE 100 and LE 200 ($30 and $60), the prospect of affording an LE 80,000 home is nothing but a fantasy.

In some areas of Cairo, land prices have increased five times over the last decade as the commodity becomes increasingly scarce. The price of raw materials has also sky-rocketed, with dealings on the black market flourishing. In addition, the lifting of many government subsidies on materials since 1992 has caused prices to double and sometimes triple.

With such unlikely prospects for acquiring decent housing, many of Cairo's urban poor have had to become imaginative in their search for shelter, and they look beyond the law. Most have resorted to informal housing. Indeed, informal housing has become not only commonplace but the norm: the Abt Associates study revealed that 80 percent of all housing units built in Cairo since 1960 had been built illegally and without permits.[12] This includes new construction as well as the vertical expansion of existing buildings. Informal housing is further encouraged by the expense of complying with legislation (that is, the lack of resources of those trying to obtain housing), the lack of knowledge of the legislation (and the lack of education of those trying to obtain housing), and the lack of enforcement of the legislation regarding informal dwellings because of corruption or neglect.

Some five to seven million of Cairo's inhabitants live in informal housing. In many cases, the dwellings resemble shantytowns and appear unfit for human habitation. It is typical on any given day for buildings to collapse in districts of informal housing.

During an earthquake (which measured 5.9 on the Richter scale) in 1992, a fourteen-story building in the wealthy suburb of Heliopolis collapsed, taking the lives of more than seventy people. The construction license for the building stated that its height should not exceed eight floors and a basement. This demonstrates how it is not only in poor areas that housing is being built informally. In the wake of the earthquake, the government has tried to stifle the construction of informal housing. Their efforts, however, have been mostly in vain.

In this century (especially in the last four decades), the deceased of the City of the Dead are increasingly sharing their resting places with the living, mostly with strangers who have no other home on earth. While there has always been a small population of people living in the cemeteries, including undertakers, guards, stone cutters, the sick, the poor, criminals, and Qu'ran reciters, the population has swelled markedly by the increasing numbers of urban poor. Accounts show that some 10,000 people were already living in the City of the Dead in 1937. By 1967, that population had grown to about 100,000. Today, as the cemeteries have increasingly become inhabited by the homeless, there could be as many as one million people living in the City of the Dead.

All types of tombs have been invaded by the homeless. Some rent out the tomb-dwellings as living quarters while others have merely taken them over. Many families try to secure their tombs against unwanted squatters, investing in locks or guards. The Egyptian Antiquities Department likewise struggles to maintain the integrity of tombs of historical significance. Increasingly, however, the locks and the will of the owners are unable to resist the demands of the poor. In some cases, the latches have been unfastened by the tomb owners themselves who, for one reason or another, found their tombs to be their only remaining source of shelter.

The invaders have adapted the tombs in creative ways to meet the needs of the living. Cenotaphs and grave markers are used as desks, headboards, tables, and shelves. String is hung between gravestones to set laundry out to dry. As in the houses of the poor elsewhere in Cairo, rooms are typically multipurpose in nature, serving as many needs as possible. The room in which the family sleeps may also be the living room, dining room, and kitchen as well. Therefore, the inhabitants eat, cook, sleep, study, and visit with friends and relatives all in the same room.

A woman dressed in traditional clothing walks through the courtyard behind her tomb-home.

Rooms are typically overcrowded, especially for sleeping. Seldom do parents have separate rooms from children, while children may have to sleep as many as seven to a bed. Many who do not have beds at all lie on carpets or on the cement or dirt floors. This is a major hardship in the winter, when the temperature drops to as low as 40° F and the floors become extremely cold. In the summer, the rooms become unbearably hot, and it is typical to see people seeking relief by sleeping outdoors.

The human inhabitants are joined by even greater numbers of cockroaches, mosquitoes, flies, and vermin of all sorts. These creatures invade every room, and are so common that the people hardly seem to notice them.

Typically, the tomb-home is also engulfed in an overwhelming stench, radiating from garbage piled up outside of the doors and windows, sewage seeping out of undrained tanks, overcrowding, and inadequate ventilation. Bathroom facilities, if they exist, are typically a two-foot square space with a cement latrine built by the inhabitants themselves. It is usually adjoined to the area that is acting as a kitchen. In both spaces, there are few or no windows, and undesirable odors inevitably linger in the house.*

As it becomes apparent to the dwellers that what was supposed to be temporary shelter may in fact be a permanent living situation, squatters will use the few resources they have available to make their tomb-dwelling into a home. Electricity may be brought into the tomb, either legally or illegally. As evidenced by the great number of wires running between the roof of Qaytbay Mosque and nearby tombs, residents tap into power lines running to mosques. A latrine or toilet may be installed; formal sewage systems are not allowed in the cemeteries, however. Furniture will be brought in, typically furniture that can serve multipurposes, such as wooden benches that can be used for sitting, eating, and sleeping. Some tomb dwellers have even been able to install running water and, on rare occasions, a telephone. Such facilities, however, are not the norm and are usually self-assembled and inefficient.**

Some areas of the cemeteries have witnessed so much growth that they now resemble other poor Cairo communities. Most of these areas tend to be around the major monuments, such as those along the street connecting the complex of Sultan Qaytbay with the complex of Sultan Barquq in the Northern Cemetery. The City is more urbanized around the Sayyida Nafisa Mosque in the Cemetery of the Great, as well as in the area surrounding the mosque and mausoleum of the Imam al-Shafi'i. Some of the tombs in these areas have one, two, or even three floors added illegally to the top of the original room or rooms. There are even some newer buildings nestled in between the tombs that house only the living and not the dead.

People living in the urbanized areas are more likely to have such amenities as electricity, running water, refrigerators, toilets, and telephones. To serve the needs of the population, grocery and convenience stores as well as cafeterias and coffee shops have crept up along the streets of the cemeteries, often in the tombs themselves.

Studies of informal housing have shown that, as squatters become more confident that they will not be run off the land, they begin to invest more of their resources into the infrastructure and ornamentation of the housing, thus creating increasingly permanent settlements. In his revolutionary book *The Other Path* (which deals with the informal sector in Peru), Hernando De Soto

---

*Many people do not have indoor bathroom facilities. Rather, holes will be dug in secluded areas behind gravestones.

**According to a May 1992 USAID Country Program Strategy 1992–1996 Report, approximately 25% of the population of Egypt have no source of treated water, and 70% do not have access to a sewerage collection system. Also, there is only a mere four telephone lines for every 100 Egyptians.

recognized that "The level of investment in housing is thus determined by the measure of legal security which the state confers on the settlement."[13] This phenomenon has occurred in the informal housing of the City of the Dead as well.

Informal housing is housing that is illegal and exists or is built in contravention of building codes and zoning laws. The inhabitants of such housing are called squatters—people who have occupied land without the permission of the owner, or who have constructed or occupied dwellings in defiance of the legislation governing the area. Officially, it is against the law to live in a cemetery. The people who have occupied the tombs of the cemeteries have done so in defiance of the law. In this sense, the community of the City of the Dead is an illegal society. It is forbidden to live in the cemeteries out of respect for the dead and by written law. It has proven difficult, however, for the legal system to prevent the urbanization of the cemeteries by living inhabitants. Whereas there are many reasons, such as the lack of means to enforce the laws, the reason most often cited by the inhabitants themselves is simple: they have no other place else to go.

Informal housing in Egypt is not unique to the City of the Dead. Construction of illegal buildings and illegal occupation of dwellings is a nationwide phenomenon. The majority of housing being created in Egypt is informal. Studies of informal housing estimate that of housing units built in Cairo between 1970 and 1981, 84 percent were informal. Studies have also found that informal housing has played a major role in allowing available housing to increase at the same rate as population growth. Informal housing, however, tends to be significantly less well equipped with infrastructure than is housing built in accordance with Egyptian codes and laws.

The informal housing of the City of the Dead is typically less crowded than housing in other informal communities because buildings in the cemeteries are generally not multi-floored. The informal housing of the cemeteries has other advantages over informal housing in different areas of Cairo as well. Residents settling in the City of the Dead invade tombs and do not have to build the initial infrastructure of their informal houses. Starting from scratch, residents of new informal communities typically have to pay to have land leveled and for initial structures to be built. Cemetery residents are able to move into pre-existing structures and improve and expand those buildings in stages as their financial situation allows.

Of course there are disadvantages of living in the City of the Dead as opposed to living in other informal communities in Cairo. Residents of the City of the Dead are insecure about the status of their residences. Unlike some informal communities that the government has come to accept, the

The Modern Era

illegal society of the cemeteries has little hope of ever being fully recognized by the government and earning an official legal status. Given this predicament, the cemetery communities have little chance of bettering their access to such services as running water, sewage, and public education and health care. Perhaps the greatest disadvantage, however, is that these people are forced to live with the dead. Death is always surrounding the people of the City of the Dead, and this takes a mental toll on residents as they are stigmatized by society and suffer discrimination based on the place in which they live. In this way, residents of the City of the Dead are set apart from other dwellers of informal housing and may be looked down upon by people living in areas much like their own, albeit without the dead.

In Cairo, informal slum dwellings provide shelter for about 45 percent of the population, with density in some areas reaching as high as 100,000 persons per square kilometer.* With such a large portion of the population living in such housing, it is easy to see how informal housing has proven to be impossible to control, especially given rising housing costs throughout Egypt.

The dramatic increases in housing costs that modern Egypt has experienced have made it extremely difficult for people to become owners or renters for the first time, or for people to change their residence. Low income families have a particularly difficult time. One study reports:

" . . . Households that have moved into a unit within the past several years are spending twice the fraction of their income on housing as average households who have not moved recently. For households in the lowest income quartile, this has meant doubling from about 15% of income to about 30% of income. With food consumption requiring between 60–70% of income among the poor, this places low income households in an extremely precarious position."[14]

Most of the residents of the City of the Dead are among the hardest of the hardest hit. They are recent immigrants to Cairo, seeking housing for the first time, and they have low incomes.

RURAL TO URBAN MIGRANTS

Most residents of the City of the Dead are first, second, or third generation immigrants from the rural areas. This is typical of inhabitants of

---

*According to the May 1992 USAID Egypt Country Program Strategy 1992–1996 Report, density in Cario averages 29,000 inhabitants per square kilometer and ranges as high as 116,000 persons per square kilometer, one of the highest concentrations of people in the world.

informal housing. Whereas 89 percent of Cairo residents who live in legal, formal housing were born in an urban area, only 53 percent of informal housing dwellers can claim that distinction. The chances that an inhabitant of Cairo is living in informal housing rises 41 percent if he or she had a rural birthplace. Thus, the informal sector is more heavily made up of migrants from the countryside than the formal sector. This may be attributed in part to the lack of knowledge of housing laws and codes by rural migrants who come from areas that are less regulated. It may also be because of lower educational levels and higher illiteracy (only 3% of people in informal housing have university degrees). The most prominent cause, however, is the lack of resources.

Rural to urban migrants can usually be categorized into two groups: selective and nonselective. Selective migrants are those who choose to move to the city, attracted by the prospect of better opportunities for education, jobs, and access to services. The city offers higher wages, increased opportunity for education, lower infant mortality, better transportation, improved communication, and increased health care services among other things. Nonselective migrants are landless peasants who come to the city out of necessity. They are the victims of the agricultural crisis. They typically have little or no education, few or no skills, and little or no savings. Both selective and nonselective migrants have been flocking to the city in enormous numbers.

Although rural migrants are attracted to the city by the perception of a better life, many fail to achieve what they expected from their migration. Instead they find that they not only have to compete with other members of the city's vast population, they have to compete against the system itself. Fundamental structural flaws in the economic system prevent them from obtaining such basic necessities as decent housing. Within such a system, legality is an option for only those with a certain degree of political and economic power. Poor migrants from the countryside quickly find themselves at the bottom of the political and economic barrel. To survive, they must look beyond the law into the world of informality.

The problem of excessive rural to urban migration has been exacerbated by a further change in migration patterns. Historically, migration would follow a two-step pattern: villagers would migrate to towns and small cities, while residents of small cities would make the move to the big city (Cairo in the case of Egypt). Contemporary patterns, however, have moved toward one step in which both villagers and small-city residents migrate directly to Cairo. As a result there has been both a dramatic increase in the numbers of rural migrants entering Cairo and a growth in the urban-rural gap. Cairo

The Modern Era

is unquestionably Egypt's leading city, far outdistancing its nearest rival in population, services, goods, wealth, and power. The capital has grown at a much faster rate than secondary cities in Egypt.

The gap between the city and the countryside has increased further as a result of the government's response to the rising problems in Cairo's housing and service industries brought about by this migration. As the government has attempted to tackle these problems, investment funds have been diverted from the smaller cities and towns and from rural areas, further increasing the existing urban-rural gap. As this gap has widened, the incentive for migration has become ever greater, creating a vicious circle that is strangling the country's economy. Mamoun Fandy, an Egyptian who grew up in a poor village in Upper Egypt writes:

> It is Misr (Cairo) where the government spends its money, builds its factories and institutes new programs. The rest of the country is economically and culturally neglected. One example epitomizes this situation: Until 1980, we did not have electricity or running water in my Upper Egyptian village; the nearest first-aid unit was 10 miles away. If your only means of transportation is donkey back, 10 miles is not a short distance. Northern towns are not any better off than the Southern ones. Therefore, if anyone from the southern or northern parts of Egypt, especially the poverty-stricken south, wants to better himself economically, he has to travel to Cairo, a foreign land for those who live outside it.[15]

Thus, migration has led to overurbanization in Egypt. That is, the urbanization that has occurred has not been matched by a corresponding or greater expansion of socio-economic conditions. Cairo has become an international symbol of overurbanization. Infrastructure, water supplies, sewage treatment, and social welfare systems in Cairo have been stretched far beyond their means as urban population growth has combined with such high rates of rural to urban migration. Jehan Sadat, wife of former President Anwar Sadat, recognized this growing phenomenon beginning in the 1970s. She wrote, "Cairo had been designed for 3 million people, but there were 9 million living there. The city's facilities were overwhelmed. Every time it rained heavily, the city sewers overflowed. The telephone circuits were so overloaded that it took 10 or 15 minutes to place a call from one side of Cairo to another."[16]

Furthermore, in many communities, instead of becoming urbanized, many rural migrants retain their rural lifestyles and trends, causing a ruralization of the city. These migrants do not readily assimilate into their new urban environment, but rather gather among other similar migrants, typically in squatter settlements such as that of the City of the Dead, maintaining much of their rural identities. Egyptian anthropologist Saad Eddin Ibrahim has observed this phenomenon, explaining that, "The heavy concentration of people from the same village or rural district shelters the new migrant from the shocks and cold impersonal environment of the big city and helps to preserve socio-cultural patterns which otherwise might be totally obliterated."[17]

People sell what land they have and go to the city in search of a better life. People whose land has gone bad (the land is increasingly failing to support the growing rural population) and landless peasants have done the same. They settle among family and friends in the cemeteries, hoping to move out of the City of the Dead after they have become established in the city. Jehan Sadat recognized this growing trend during her husband's presidency. She wrote:

> Migration from the villages made Cairo's problems especially severe. Falaheen (peasant farmers) seeking a better life for themselves and their families were streaming into Ramesses railroad station so constantly that the number of people living in the city went up by 1 person every 90 seconds. Many of the new arrivals could find no place to live, and they built make-shift sheds on rooftops or in alleyways. More than half a million others moved permanently to the City of the Dead, setting up Entire communities complete with shops and cafes among the mausoleums.[18]

For many, the initial shock of living in the city is compounded by the shocking conditions of much of the cemeteries. Even those who join relatives and friends in the cemeteries are surprised by what they find, as few men return to the villages admitting that they were not better off as a result of their migration. Yet many of them are not. In his study of Peru, Hernando De Soto writes:

> The poor have fled from the countryside to the cities. When these poor . . . reached the city, they found that the system had already closed its door on them. They had no money and no technical training. They had no hope of getting credit, no chance to obtain insurance, and could expect no protection from the police or the judicial system. They knew their businesses would always be threatened from all sides. All they had was their will, their imagination, and their desire to work.[19]

The same is true of Egypt's rural migrants.

The similarities in lifestyle and traditions between rural villages and the City of the Dead are evident in all aspects of life in the cemeteries: from the way the household is run and organized to the way family members interact with each other and with outsiders. Indeed, in some areas of the cemetery, it appears as if entire villages have been uprooted and transplanted among the graves. Neighbors have often traveled from the same rural areas to settle in the City of the Dead. And often numerous units of extended families are living side by side. They do indeed (as noted by Saad E. Ibrahim) offer a support group that makes the transition from rural to urban life less traumatic. New migrants find it very important to live near relatives or friends. Egyptians seldom think of themselves as individuals. Rather, they see themselves in relation to others; family, friends, and members of the same social class. In fact, their proximity to friends or relatives is often a major factor in a migrant's choice of an initial place to settle, and tends to override even the advantages of settling where there is easy access to such services as education and health care. Rural Egyptian society is very family oriented. An individual is identified with his family name and his or her family has a reputation well-known by society. Migration limits the importance of family association. Family networks are gradually replaced by networks of co-workers and neighbors. However, by settling beside relatives or migrants from the same village, family identification retains its importance. Even after having lived in an area such as the City of the Dead, if a family accumulates enough money to allow them to move to another, more well-equipped area, they may be reluctant to leave family and friends behind.

Although their surroundings are different, the migrants from the countryside resist changes in their activities and in attitude. A walk through the cemeteries reveals households with rooms organized to serve multiple purposes as they are in the villages. There are not the strict functions for different areas that are typical of urban households. In essence, what is available is made to serve the greatest number of functions possible. Also, it is common to see animals such as chickens, ducks, pigeons and even goats and lambs being raised by families in the cemeteries. They will be scattered in the courtyards, on the roofs of buildings, and even inside the buildings themselves, often competing with people for the available space. Family members will sit in doorways and greet passers by with *salaam aleikum* (God's peace be with you) and *idfaddal* (please come in). The people of the City of the Dead are generally inviting or indifferent to outsiders. Even the occasional foreigner who winds his way through the City of the Dead will usually be greeted with friendliness and curiosity, and they will often be asked to sit down and share a cup of tea.

NONRURAL TO URBAN MIGRANTS

Today, the population of the City of the Dead is growing as much from internal growth as from rural migration. The number of new residents who originate from other parts of Cairo match the new migrants from the countryside. Indeed, living alongside the rural migrants of the City of the Dead are more established urban dwellers who are there as victims of Cairo's housing crisis. Given the shoddy building practices, it is not unusual for houses to collapse in poorer areas of Cairo, leaving the residents in the streets with few earthly belongings. While they may be promised new housing by the government, most have to wait a considerable amount of time until such housing becomes available. Given little or no other choice, such families will move into the cemeteries for temporary shelter. More often than not, government promises fail to materialize and the lack of other opportunities persist. Thus, as in the case of the rural migrant, what was thought to be a transient situation often becomes permanent.

These victims of Cairo's fragile infrastructure are joined by other urban dwellers who, for one reason or another, have found themselves without affordable housing. As a last resort, they settle in the cemeteries. Sometimes their family has a burial plot they are able to move in to. More often, however, they find themselves invading a tomb, or renting that tomb from the owners. Other inhabitants of the City of the Dead are descendants or families of the guardians of tombs and of *hanoutis*, those people who oversee large areas of a cemetery. Some of these inhabitants continue to perform the duties of their predecessors. Others have taken up additional economic activities as a means of earning a living. Still others have rented the tombs that they had kept watch over as their duties have become irrelevant. Many have taken key money from prospective tomb-dwellers (money in exchange for the key to the tomb), thereby allowing families to move into tombs that they once protected from encroachment.

An important subcommunity of the City of the Dead moved there after the 1967 War turned the Sinai Peninsula into a battlefield between Egypt and Israel and drove many of its Egyptian residents to Cairo. Immigrants also came from the Suez Canal cities, which were largely destroyed during the war. At this time, the housing crunch was just beginning to explode in the capital city. The crisis exacerbated the difficulty of obtaining affordable housing. During and immediately after the 1967 War, Egypt's resources were sunk into the war effort. As a result, few resources went toward maintaining Cairo's infrastructure. Soon, this infrastructure could no longer accommodate the rapidly expanding population. Many of those with little money found themselves settling in the cemetery. In the wake of the war, the government built some low-cost housing units for refugees in the area around Qaytbay Mosque in the Northern Cemetery. Ironically, they would come to live beside some of the young men who lost their lives trying to protect their homes and the land of the Sinai. A War Cemetery (also known as the Martyr's Cemetery) that houses soldiers from the 1967 and 1973 wars was built by the government at the northern tip of the City of the Dead beside the Mosque and Mausoleum of the Sultan Barquq.

The cemetery also has been and remains a place where many newly married couples begin their lives together. The price of getting married has risen so high that, in Cairo, the average age of marriage is now around 35 for men and 30 for women. Young people cannot afford to get married. Ahmed El-Ghamri of *Al-Ahram Weekly* commented, "Marriage has become a luxury that only the rich can contemplate without panic. The future is dim. Fewer and fewer young men can afford to provide their bride with even the smallest flat and the bare necessities to start a life together."[20] With little savings and barely enough money to afford marriage itself, many newly married couples seek inexpensive shelter in the City of the Dead. Some couples have been living with the groom's family and move to the cemeteries when they decide to begin a family of their own. They hope that their stay in the City of the Dead will be short. Many such couples, however, find that their temporary refuge becomes their permanent home as they find no affordable way out of the cemeteries.

Some rare tomb-dwellers of the City of the Dead have willfully chosen to make the cemetery their homes. This was the case of Mamdouh Abbass' family (see p. 84). These people feel a very strong bond with one or more of the family's dead. They will spend religious holidays and feasts (especially the Ramadan feast) at the tomb in honor of and thanksgiving with the deceased. Eventually, that bond causes the family to choose to make the tomb their permanent or semi-permanent residence. These families will usually have many of the amenities of modern-day life, such as electricity, running water, television, refrigerators, and toilets. Often, their tombs are more comfortably equipped than slum housing in other parts of Cairo.

SEX ROLES & FAMILY LIFE

As in the villages, strictly defined sex roles are the norm in the City of the Dead, with the men's sphere of influence being outside of the home or the public sphere and the women's realm being the home or the private sphere. These spheres touch but seldom overlap. Even friendship between unrelated adult men and women and young adults of the opposite sex is virtually prohibited.

Both men and women are largely defined by the roles that they play in family life. Men are first and foremost fathers and have the ultimate responsibility for providing for their family. They are seen as the breadwinners and financial planners. They are the authority figures and act with great independence. In the family hierarchy, the father commands while the mother and children obey. In traditional Egypt, if a family is seen as being needy by their relatives and friends, the father is seen by others (and usually by himself) as not succeeding in his duties toward his family. This perception exists in the cemetery communities. In the City of the Dead, however, men are typically judged against one another and not against men in society in general. To do the latter would condemn all men of the City of the Dead to failure. Rather, men are succeeding in their duties if they are providing a better life for their families than their neighbors or friends. In fact, more emphasis is typically put on a man fulfilling his financial duties than his emotional duties to his family. A man who may not demonstrate love for his family but who provides for them in financial terms, is considered a successful father by society. This phenomenon is demonstrated in the personalities of the characters in Naguib Mahfouz's *Palace Walk*. Mahfouz is a Nobel Prize-winning Egyptian author whose stories typically are set in traditional Egypt. Ahmed Abd al-Jawad, a leading character in the novel, plays a father who provides well for his family but is feared by his wife and children. By society's standards, he is a model father. Similar to Abd al-Jawad, many of the men of the cemetery communities also have strikingly different personalities when dealing with friends as opposed to their families. Men will often be stern and emotionless with family members (especially women and children), yet free spirited with their male companions.

Men are expected to socialize with other men, and they will usually gather in coffee houses or in homes to enjoy *sheesha* (the smoking of the waterpipe) and conversation. One typical criticism of these men is that they will frequently spend what little money they have on socializing, cigarettes, or sheesha while their families go without basic necessities.* There are numerous coffee houses in the more urbanized areas of the cemeteries which teem with men long into the night. Older men will sit dressed in the traditional garb of Egyptians: a flowing *galabeya* and a scarf wrapped

---

*A man who smokes a pack of local cigarettes per day would spend about 44 LE per month. This is a large chunk of a monthly salary. As noted, an average monthly salary is 100–200 LE and is frequently much lower among residents of the cemeteries.

around the head, or in tan safari-like suits. They sit, talk about the way things used to be, and watch the people passing by. The young, some clad in galabeyas while others don more western-style clothing, play backgammon or dominoes, and will discuss the problems of modern-day life, wondering out loud about where they will find work, how they can save the money needed to marry, and how they will be able to provide for their families.

In the winter, the men often assemble in the streets or in pathways between the tombs, sitting around large metal bowls filled with earth and corn cobs, which are burnt for warmth. It is expected that men will spend most of their free time outside of the home. The inside of the home is seen as the place where women socialize and men are not expected to spend their time with the women. Men who spend a significant amount of time at home with their families may be ridiculed by other men and have their masculinity questioned.

Another reason these men socialize outside of their homes is that they are embarrassed to bring their friends home and reveal the conditions in which they live. This is especially true if a man has a friend from outside of the cemeteries. In cases such as these, the men may even lie about the area where they live. Lower class Egyptians frequently place a high value on material possessions. Therefore, socializing away from home is a way for a man who is not materially well off to protect his pride. When men do assemble in the home, they are usually relatives or close friends. As the men sit and talk, women will always be prepared to fill their orders for tea, fruit, or whatever is available.

As in the Egyptian countryside, women of the City of the Dead adhere to a strict system of sexual segregation and a rigid code of conduct, a system that is valued and perpetuated by each succeeding generation of girls. Anthropologist Helen Watson writes that, "At the core of this conviction is the perception that gender roles and male and female responsibilities are fully complementary. There is a male sphere of influence and activity and a female one; both are separate and distinct, but in combination they form the basis of a stable society."[21]

Women are expected to complement the men by being patient, resourceful, and willing to fulfill the needs of others. A woman's major responsibilities are motherhood, loyalty, and the management of domestic affairs. A woman's life is supposed to be private, secluded from the outside world. Most families of the City of the Dead, however, do not have the resources that this ideal role for women would require. Still, women do not venture into the streets very often. If a woman does have to go out in public, she will usually be accompanied by her husband or another relative, an adult friend, or her children. Black, long-sleeved, full-length robes cover the clothes that she wears in the home. A black head scarf covers her hair. Her tasks will be carried out quickly. Loitering in public places could bring criticism from neighbors. Still, it is not uncommon to see women sitting in the doorways of the tombs in which they live. They can be seen washing clothes, shelling peas, cleaning rice, rocking babies, or simply socializing with other women or family members. This practice and its widespread acceptance by the people of the City of the Dead may appear surprising. Indeed, such actions would not be accepted in many other informal Cairo communities. Although many women of the City of the Dead would not dare sit in full view of the public and criticize those women who do, most of the women did not see this as a violation of the rigid code of conduct expected of women of the City of the Dead. When considering that in rural Egypt the doorstep is seen as an active part of the household where numerous activities are conducted, the practice of doorsitting in the City of the Dead is more understandable. Given the rural backgrounds of most of the inhabitants of the cemeteries, it is natural that this practice should be accepted.

All domestic work is the duty of women. This includes cleaning, cooking, washing, and looking after the children. Women are expected to fulfill the needs of the men of the house, to whom they are expected to be obedient. Often, during meals, the men will eat first, and the women will eat what is left over—especially when guests are present. Typically, family members will sit on a plastic rug on the floor and gather around a large aluminum tray or a short, round wooden table. Dining rooms with tables and chairs do not exist in the City of the Dead. The meal might consist of, depending on what the family can afford, a mound of white rice, green salad, bread and cheese, with occasional meat and soup.* At the end of the meal (again, especially when guests are present), a woman will bring around a bowl with soap and water for the men to wash their hands. The man will hold his hands over the basin while the woman pours water over them.

Though common, this description of activities exists only in those households that have the resources to support such activities. Many households do not, and those that do are unlikely to have such resources at their disposal on a daily basis. In fact, one of the elements of the communities of

---

*People of the City of the Dead occasionally have to go for days without eating in order to conserve, or they may have only rice or only beans. Frequently, it is the women and children who make such sacrifices. When there is meat, it usually consists of one or two small pieces per person.

the City of the Dead that is most surprising, is the great differences in the amount of resources that families have at their disposal. There are countless families who do not know if they will have food from one day to the next, frequently depending on the charity of others. On the opposite end of the spectrum, there are families who always seem to be able to fill the plates and the stomachs of all those present. These families, however, are certainly not the norm in the City of the Dead.

While the men are away at work, women will often gather in small groups within the tomb-homes or on doorsteps. In their groups, the women will spend hours talking and commiserating about the lives they lead, the cost of living, their husbands, and other people living in the area. Gossiping is a primary source of entertainment for the women of the City of the Dead, and they are always looking for a new piece of news. The smallest details take on great importance as they are repeated over and over again. Talk about money, food, and husbands typically dominates the conversation. The women will relate exactly what they have eaten that day and the cost of each item. Then, they will fantasize about what they would love to be able to eat. Similarly, they will compare what time their husbands came home, as well as any money or any gifts the men brought them. A husband's love for his wife in this society is often measured in the amount of material things that he provides for her (the same manner in which the man is judged as being successful or not). Women will complain about the money their husbands squander on cigarettes and in the coffee houses. Talk may also turn to neighbors who are not part of the select group of women who are gathered. Gossiping will ensue. This allows these women to compare themselves favorably to the other women of the area.*

As stated earlier, many of the women will sit in their doorways and observe everything that is taking place in the street outside. They usually combine this with the performance of a household task such as shelling peas. A woman who has a task at hand appears more respectful than a woman whose sole objective is to observe (and, others will claim, to be observed). Women look to see who is visiting with whom, whose husband is coming home with a package for his family (the women are frequently jealous of each other and try to prove that they have more than their neighbors; if a neighbor is obviously better off, women often resort to criticism of morals)** and they listen for quarrels among neighbors. All that

---

*This is common of poor women in Cairo. I recognized this trend after reading Unni Wikan's study of Cairo's poor. See Unni Wikan, *Life Among the Poor in Cairo*.
**This is also noted in Unni Wikan's book, *Life Among the Poor in Cario*.

is seen by the door-sitters is later related to the other women at evening gatherings.*

Women and girls in traditional Egypt learn early in life that their role is to be a mother and a wife. Nothing evokes the excitement, happiness, and jealously among girls more than the announcement that some lucky young woman has become engaged (except, perhaps, the birth of a son). Marriage and childbearing are seen as the primary functions of girls and women, the sources of her status in society. In fact, when a woman gives birth to a son, she no longer is known by her own name. Instead, she becomes known as *Om* _____ or *Mother of*_____ (her son's name). This is common among traditional Egyptians, and it is not limited to the people of the City of the Dead.

The cost of marriage in Egypt is great when compared to wages. Low income Egyptians will often go without food or other basic necessities in order to save their limited resources for a child's wedding. Often, engagements are extended for years to give the families time to finance the marriages. Marriage in the City of the Dead is not a contract between two individuals. Rather, it is a contract between two families (or within the same family) that it is hoped will strengthen bonds and enhance the respect and public image of the families. Arranged marriages are common. Marriages for love are not.

As in rural Egypt (especially Upper Egypt), some of the most desirable marriages take place between cousins. Many of the older women of the City of the Dead who had been born in rural Egypt had married their cousins when they were very young. This agreement had been made within the family and the two individuals directly involved had little, if any, say in the matter. Today, for families in the City of the Dead, it is more difficult to arrange marriage between cousins as many families are recent migrants to Cairo who left their extended families behind in the villages. Still, marriages between cousins are preferred. Single men from the City of the Dead may travel back to the places of their rural roots to find a bride and then return with her to live in the cemeteries.

Traditional Egyptians consider the ideal mate for a man to be his father's brother's daughter; for a woman, her mother's sister's son would be the ideal.** Choosing a spouse is a family affair. Individuals seldom, as with other important decisions in life, choose a spouse alone.

---

*I also noted this among village women during my time spent in rural Egypt.
**For further explanation see Andrea Rugh's book, *Family Life in Contemporary Egypt.*

One exception to this rule in the City of the Dead is the case of Mamdouh Abbass and his second wife. Mamdouh announced to his family that he was going to marry Sandy, a Canadian living in Cairo. He had made this decision without consulting other family members, but he went to great lengths to ensure her acceptance. For their part, family members interviewed Sandy at length to be sure that this was not merely an irrational love relationship, but that Sandy and Mamdouh had complementary characteristics that would help to ensure the success of the marriage. Also, Mamdouh's relatives wanted to be sure that Sandy understood the responsibilities she was taking on as the wife of a Muslim Egyptian man, and they judged her ability to fulfill such responsibilities. The acceptance of Sandy by Mamdouh's family was made easier because the family realized the opportunities afforded Mamdouh by marrying a foreigner. Sandy, however, had to overcome the stereotype of Western women being morally bankrupt, which many Egyptians firmly believe.

In performing their roles as wives and mothers, these women's primary concerns are economic. They are required to be thrifty and resourceful. Questions always weigh on their minds: How am I going to feed the children? Where do I find blankets? How do I get the children to school? Where will the shoes come from? How can I contribute to the family economy? Women of the City of the Dead are also concerned with social issues: If I don't bear my husband a son will he take another wife? What if my husband doesn't respect me? Who will I find to marry my children? Westerners searching for a revolutionary potential among the women of the City of the Dead will be disappointed. The issues that dominate their lives are not political. They are issues of everyday life and survival.

Describing the position of women in the City of the Dead, Helen Watson writes:

> Men and women do not mix freely. Women keep at a distance from men as much as possible and dress in the familiar body-concealing clothes, while men crowd the coffee houses and public places. There are few women who appear at ease in the streets. A high value is placed on female modesty, and this explains many of the restrictions on women's freedom of movement, conduct, style of dress and so on. Female virginity is the sine qua non of marriage, and marriage itself is the universal goal. On these two accounts alone it is vital for a woman to avoid any charge of immodest behaviour, since this would impair her marriage prospects.[22]

While women from the countryside will attempt to preserve many of their rural attitudes and customs, they are forced to confront the reality that they are living in a new, different, and often more hostile environment. Whereas in their villages they tended to view waged work outside of the home as men's work, many of the women of the City of the Dead find themselves compelled to contribute to the family economy. Most are working for wages for the first time. This creates tension, as waged work is typically seen as a source of disgrace for women and shame for their husbands, who are labeled as unable to provide for their families. For married women, waged work is considered a last resort and does not have a place in the rigid code of conduct required of women by traditional Egyptian society—a society that doesn't allow men and women to mix freely. Public waged labor requires a woman to sacrifice the high level of public modesty considered desirable. Compromising modest behavior can prove detrimental to the marriage prospects of unmarried girls—a fate desired by none. Women also fear that waged work may prevent them from fulfilling their household responsibilities. In some cases, however, work becomes a necessary evil. Nevertheless, a married woman who is working to help provide food or other necessities for the family will sometimes even try to hide the fact that she is working from her husband in order to spare his pride. Women who suddenly find themselves widowed or divorced are forced to take on such responsibilities for mere survival.

There are different levels of acceptance of work among the women of the City of the Dead. Women who participate in such activities as sewing piecework in their homes are usually not punished for these actions. Rather, such work is seen as an extension of their household duties. The sale of items from inside or in front of the tomb-home is grudgingly accepted. Young girls frequently work outside of the home, but they are expected to stop when they become engaged. Married women working outside of the home for wages is not accepted. Although Egyptian women have been entering Egypt's workforce in growing numbers, the City of the Dead is home to few career-minded women and girls, and there appears to be very little change in that direction.

To avoid working, women may try to make ends meet by borrowing from family and friends. If a woman borrows, however, she frequently must also hide this act from her husband. Like working, borrowing is considered to be a shameful act, demonstrating that the husband has been unable to provide for his family. Borrowing from other family members is more accepted than borrowing from nonfamily members. In Egypt, extended family members are expected to help their relatives in their times of need.

Women of the City of the Dead may also resort to selling their material possessions. It is not uncommon for a woman to sell the gold bracelets, earrings, or rings she received from her husband as wedding gifts. Sometimes even everyday items such as kitchen utensils, pots and pans, and furniture must be sold. Families will also try to save money by not celebrating occasions that call for large expenses, such as Islamic feasts, the birth of a child, or a child's circumcision. According to Egyptian tradition, gifts should be given on such occasions. Families with few resources at their disposal, however, may be forced to refuse such gifts so that they will not be obligated to reciprocate. At the feast celebrating the end of Ramadan, some families may stay indoors while most families parade the streets with their new clothes and shoes.

CHILDREN

President Mubarak has proclaimed 1989–99 to be the Decade for the Protection and Development of the Egyptian Child. In spite of this, child labor has been on the rise in Egypt. There are currently about 1.5 million children under the age of fifteen working in jobs from sweeping floors to mixing chemicals, accounting for about 10 percent of Egypt's total labor force. CAPMAS, an Egyptian agency responsible for collecting statistical data, estimates that 71.1 percent of children work in agricultural and desert regions and 30 percent work in urban centers. Between 1974 and 1984 alone, there was almost a 300 percent increase in the number of working children between the ages of six and twelve. Moreover, the startling high official figures on child labor in Egypt do not take into account the additional thousands in the informal sector. Growing numbers of street children can be seen selling tissues, gathering rubbish, or simply begging for food and money. One report noted that many of these street children, "find employment collecting cigarette butts and then reselling them. The same is done with plastic and cardboard. Most beg, however, and a few have to sell themselves. A day of begging can earn LE 5, and an hour of homosexual activity LE 10 or more."[23]

A report in the *Cairo Papers for Social Science*, a periodical of the American University in Cairo, showed that working children typically come from "poor backgrounds, belong to large families, and were hired through family or neighborhood connections rather than through the employment bureaux."[24] For many Egyptian children, especially those from low income areas such as the City of the Dead, childhood does not last long. Children are forced to grow up and accept adult responsibilities at a very young age.

One of the first things that strikes any visitor to the City of the Dead is the conditions in which children play, work, and grow. An outsider entering the cemeteries will probably be immediately surrounded by a mob of them, dressed in tattered clothing and without shoes, reaching out their soiled hands and excitedly asking for pens or money. They can be aggressive in their approach, grabbing on to arms or legs. Some of them do this to intimidate. Most do it out of genuine need and a belief that the more fortunate should give to those who have less. Their cry for pens may seem surprising, but is evidence of how even the most basic of school supplies is often unaffordable. Why not ask for money instead of pens? The children are afraid that the money would be confiscated by parents and used for an alternative purpose.

Families in the cemeteries (as in the villages) tend to be larger than formal-sector, urban families. Many women are uninformed about birth control, cannot afford it, are afraid, or refuse to use such devices. Like village women, many of the women of the City of the Dead choose to have large families. Large numbers of children provide a woman with a sort of status among her friends and neighbors. Children provide an extra source of income as they get older and are able to work. They become a kind of social security for women. Also, a man is less likely to divorce a wife if he has a large family that he'll have to continue to support, another incentive for a woman to have many children. Over the last two years, however, the men and women of the City of the Dead are increasingly recognizing the disadvantages of having large families. Discussions on the subject were common among both men and women of the City of the Dead during the International Conference on Population and Development held in Cairo in September 1994, which was widely covered by the Egyptian media. Both traditional and progressive opinions were voiced by cemetery residents, with traditional views still gaining more support. The fact that such issues are being discussed, however, shows that government campaigns to control population are reaching some of the groups on the periphery of Egyptian society.

What does it mean to be a child in the City of the Dead? It means that you have started your life in a position of extreme disadvantage. For you, most of the doors to opportunity and self-fulfillment are closed: education, legal employment, legal housing. Your childhood is short-lived. There are no playgrounds, no parks, and few open spaces in the City of the Dead where you can play with your friends. The rubbish-strewn streets and alleys are your only playground. You and your friends play among the garbage and sewage collecting between the tombs. You remember one friend who

The Modern Era

Two girls play in a gutted-out wardrobe in the Bab al-Nasr Cemetery.

accidentally stepped on a piece of metal while playing football. A week later, he was dead (one out of every eight children in Egypt dies before they reach the age of five). You thank God you have shoes.*

If your parents can afford to send you to school, it will probably only be for a few initial years during which you will be packed into overcrowded classrooms with teachers who serve their time in the public school classrooms but rely on private lessons as their real source of income. As you get older, you see that only those whose parents can afford such lessons are succeeding. For the rest, literacy seems an impossible goal, and you watch as one by one, the children like you fall through the cracks.

After a few years in school, your parents also decide that you are more useful providing for the family. The supplies for your education drain limited family resources, and you do not seem to be benefiting from your

---

*According to a May 1992 USAID Egypt Country Program Strategy 1992–1996 Report, Egyptian children continue to die from preventable causes in great numbers. Acute respiratory infections 28%, diarrhea 27%, and complications of pregnancy 13% are the top killers. The maternal mortality rate is high at 260 per 100,000.

time spent in school. They decide that it would be better if you learned to work. You become a young adult at the age of seven.*

If you are lucky, your father makes an agreement with a friend who owns a coffee house beside the tomb. You will serve tea (*shey*) and coffee (*ahwa*), and you will soon learn how to prepare *sheesha*. You work eight hours a day, seven days a week, and you will be paid about LE 30 every month (less than $10). The money that you make will help to pay for the marriages of your two sisters.

Your friends are also working but are less fortunate, forced to work twelve and sixteen hour shifts repairing cars as assistants to mechanics or running machinery in make-shift factories. You discover that some of the older boys find jobs delivering drugs to customers outside the cemetery. One boy has participated in homosexual activities for money. Still older boys are rumored to be joining fundamentalist groups and are training to carry out violent activities against the government. You know that you will also be faced with these possibilities as you grow older. What direction will you take?

Your sister, a year younger than you, also left school recently. According to your mother, your sister will receive more appropriate lessons by staying at home and your mother will be her teacher. She will learn the day-to-day activities of running a household, and she will relieve your mother of some of her tasks. She must become keen in these activities so that a favorable marriage can be arranged.

Another sister, three years older, has already mastered the running of a household, and relatives are talking about what a wonderful bride she will make for your cousin. Last week, relatives gathered in your home to celebrate her circumcision.** You remember your sister's piercing screams as a neighborhood woman performed the operation. You wanted to reach out and help her, but you were confused by the cries of joy from the rest of the family.

You have been told that after your sister's marriage, she will leave to join another family. Your second sister will follow the same path. You, however, must stay and eventually take over the responsibilities of the household. You

---

*Children under 12 years of age comprise some 7 percent of Egypt's labor force.

**It is my opinion that female circumcision is widely practiced in the City of the Dead. I never opened the subject with women or girls in the City of the Dead, however. For me to discuss such a topic with them would be considered a rude invasion of their privacy. It would not be accepted. In 1994, however, when CNN caused a controversy by airing the circumcision of an Egyptian girl, I was able to discuss the subject with many men. Most believed that this practice was religious and required of all Muslims.

will provide finances, and you will support your parents in their old age. You will also look after your married sisters to ensure their well-being. You dream of moving your family to another area or traveling to another country but realize, even at your young age, that dreams seldom come true in the City of the Dead.

ECONOMICS

The original inhabitants of the City of the Dead worked as tomb keepers for wealthy Cairo families. In the early twentieth century, many of the men of the Northern Cemetery worked in nearby lime kilns. In the Southern Cemetery, men often worked in the lime quarries that were close by. These trades continued to provide employment for the City of the Dead's men through the middle of the century. Janet Abu-Lughod records that in 1947, "Mining and quarrying still accounted for the largest proportion of employed males in each and every tract in the district [the City of the Dead], with services (presumably custodial care of the tombs) also important in the larger cemeteries."[25] Still, as the population continued to grow, these two trades could not accommodate the increasing number of men seeking work. Men had to look for work elsewhere. Abu-Lughod notes that by the middle of the century, "Employment was more diversified than before and could not be accounted for by the limited opportunities of the local vicinity. Men were engaged in transportation, in trade, in construction, and even in personal services. . . . By 1960 . . . specialization of the labor force had virtually disappeared."[26]

Today, the people of the City of the Dead are involved in a variety of economic activities. Some residents have secured low-paying jobs in the formal sector of Cairo's economy. These positions may be in a private office, in the transportation sector, as unskilled labor, or in entry-level government jobs. A few residents have been able to set up small informal businesses such as kiosks, food stands, or coffee shops (mostly in the cemeteries themselves). Numerous other residents of the City of the Dead are among the ranks of Cairo's unemployed. Migration has transferred rural unemployment into increased urban unemployment. Many of the residents of the cemeteries do not hold one specific occupation for any length of time. Men float from temporary job to temporary job, making money wherever money is to be made. In most cases, the people of the City of the Dead (as they have done in their search for shelter) find creative means of employment in the informal economy. They sell tissues or vegetables in the streets, wipe the dirt and dust off of car windshields, shine shoes at coffee houses, or hawk newspapers.

Similar to informal housing, the informal economy consists of those economic activities that are not officially noticed through registration and taxation procedures. They are distinguished from formal economic activities that are licensed and take place in institutionalized hierarchies. Informal sector activities range from individual actions such as hawking on streetcorners to small-scale enterprises. The members of the informal economic sector are typically from marginalized groups of society such as those of the City of the Dead. Indeed, informal economic activity and informal housing frequently go hand-in-hand. It is estimated that more than half of informal sector workers live in informal housing. Informal economic activity is usually characterized by the unreliability of employment as well as by low social mobility. The informal sector, however, does provide some sort of economic activity for an ever-growing portion of the population. One study published in the *Cairo Papers for Social Science* determined that this system "helps explain the Egyptian miracle—the day-to-day survival of large numbers of people."[27]

Much informal economic activity is taking place within the City of the Dead's borders. As mentioned previously, informal shops have been created in the cemeteries, providing services to the cemeteries's residents. Traveling salesmen traverse the streets and alleys yelling out the names of their wares, and young boys selling bottled gas walk along banging a wrench on the bottle's side to let everyone know they are coming. Hawkers calling out the names of their wares allow the women of the City of the Dead to purchase many of their daily needs close to home. There are even make-shift factories in the cemeteries, often noticeable by the streams of black smoke rising among the tombs. In one such factory in the Northern Cemetery, young boys work at machinery making aluminum bowls. The children are covered from head to foot with black soot and are frequently working without adult supervision. A few minutes away, young boys and men repair and repaint cars among the tombs. Others wait alongside the Autostrade Highway to fill the tires of trucks passing.

Walking between the mausolea of the Sultan Barquq and the Sultan Qaytbay in the northern area of the City of the Dead, it is hard to believe that this area is inside a cemetery. Not only is the street home to multitudes of tomb-dwellers, but interspersed among them are three barbers, a makeshift restaurant, two coffee houses, a shoe store, a factory, and even a jewelry store displaying silver in its windows.

There are also various markets in the cemeteries that attract visitors and vendors from various parts of Cairo. Beside the mausoleum of the Imam al Shafi'i in the Southern Cemetery, a popular market is held every Friday. Here, Egyptians and a few adventurous foreigners can be seen bartering for antiques—from coffee grinders to telephones, cameras to phonographs. Not far away, also in the Southern Cemetery, there is a bird and animal market that is a favorite among Cairenes. Here, animals, birds, fish, cages, and animal feed are displayed by vendors spread out over the streets and alleyways.

INFRASTRUCTURE, HEALTH CARE, AND EDUCATION

Like the majority of Egyptians, the government of Egypt has also largely chosen to ignore the situation of the masses living in the City of the Dead, perhaps with the hope that the problems would simply fade away. The situation has only worsened, however. Unable to provide a quick alternative to these illegal informal housing communities, the government has been forced to extend some services into the cemeteries over the years. There are now public water taps in some areas, along with community telephones and post offices. Where public taps are nonexistent, residents of the City must buy water from vendors who drive through the cemeteries in trucks or receive water from nearby mosques. For most residents of the City of the Dead, maintaining an adequate water supply is a difficult and time-consuming task. Women and girls spend considerable amounts of time fetching water, which must be stored in barrels, pots, and pans.

Formal sewage systems are still rare in the cemetery. Residents who have any sewage facilities usually have make-shift latrines with holding tanks for the disposal of toilet waste. Tanks are often left undrained, however, and sewage spills into the streets. When they are drained, the waste frequently ends up in the street anyway as residents simply empty the tanks into nearby open spaces. Most residents cannot afford to have the tanks emptied by tanker vehicles, and they have little alternative but to dump the contents close by. This causes a severe health risk as children frequently play beside these dump sites. Furthermore, many of the residents have no sewage facilities at all and are forced to use holes dug behind gravestones.

As proof of government efforts to improve the quality of life for residents of the City of the Dead, more and more residents have gained access to electricity and telephones. Public buses now traverse many of the cemeteries' larger streets, or at least come in close proximity to the cemeteries. Roads officially recognized by the government are kept paved and the cemeteries have become more secure with increased police presence. Like-

A group of girls gather water from the public tap in the Northern Cemetery.

wise, there have been attempts to improve the sanitary conditions in the City. These efforts, however, have largely fallen short of their goals and the streets, paths, and alleys of the City of the Dead are typically littered with garbage and debris. Many parts of the cemeteries have no formal system of garbage removal. The *zabaleen*, informal collectors of the majority of Cairo's waste, prefer to avoid poorer areas where the garbage is less valuable for recycling (from which most of the zabaleen's income is made). Garbage is often dumped along the sides of streets and in vacant areas, and it is eventually burned by residents.

The unsanitary conditions in the City of the Dead allow sickness and disease to flourish. The overcrowding, the lack of garbage and sewage disposal, the lack of water and cleaning materials, the lack of refrigeration of foods, the weather conditions (stifling heat in the summer, damp and cold in the winter), the proximity of animals (which often live in the same rooms as the people), and the large numbers of insects and rodents provide prime conditions for the spread of disease. Malnourishment is also widespread as many diets lack protein.

The Modern Era

Access to affordable health care is severely limited. Most residents of the cemeteries live in fear of falling seriously ill. With little or no savings, they cannot afford the luxury of decent health care. Many residents will not go to see a doctor until they simply can no longer bear the pain they are suffering. Serious illnesses will go untreated, often resulting in death. Other residents who have grave sicknesses that are not fatal typically have to travel well outside the cemeteries to receive any kind of medical attention. Likewise, medical supplies must be brought into the cemeteries from outside. Many of the traditional residents will rely on the advice of pharmacists and other family members in order to avoid doctor's fees. Government subsidized health care does exist. As with people in other informal communities in Egypt, however, the people tend not to trust it. Many people believe that any doctor who would work in such an establishment must be poorly trained and educated. If this were not the case, they feel, such a doctor would have secured a higher paying position in the private sector. This attitude reflects the general mistrust of low income Egyptians of any services provided by the government.

For others, even the subsidized care is too expensive. Many people save their money so that they can consult private doctors when they fall seriously ill. There are, however, charlatans who make a living taking advantage of such people. These so-called physicians will go to the cemeteries and present people with false credentials and walk off with their meager savings, leaving them with worthless or even harmful medical advice.

Men fear falling ill and ask how, in such cases, can they provide for their families. Many of them are already supporting elderly parents who need frequent medical care and expensive medication, including Arabe and Mamdouh Abbass (see pp. 81 and 84). Both of Mamdouh Abbass' parents had recurring medical problems that were a drain on Mamdouh's and his father's incomes. Mamdouh himself was frequently bedridden with back problems. For years he put off having an operation for lack of adequate funds. Mamdouh's family doesn't trust government health care. Rather, they insist on saving their limited resources to consult with private physicians. When Azza, one of Mamdouh's sisters, was pregnant with her first child, she insisted on having the baby at a private hospital and paying about ten times the cost of a delivery in a government health care facility. Azza would be considered foolish by some and lucky by others. Indeed, most mothers-to-be in the City of the Dead receive little, if any, prenatal care. The majority of births take place at home. Similarly, post-natal care is virtually nonexistent unless a baby appears to be sick. Such facts go a long way in explaining the high infant mortality rates among Egypt's poorer classes.

In recent years, Egypt has become a hotbed of organ transplants from live donors, most often members of the urban poor. In transplant procedures, patients and donors are taken into the operating room side by side and undergo the surgery. Most clients in these procedures are wealthy Persian Gulf Arabs. Whereas there are other countries in the Middle East that have transplant centers, few of them have the enormous numbers of poor who are willing to sell their organs. In the past, laboratories would send recruiters into Cairo's slums and poor areas (such as the City of the Dead) to enlist potential donors.

Like health care, education is another area of concern for residents of the City of the Dead. Many of the cemeteries' residents find the costs of education too great. Although there is Qu'ran instruction that is attended by many of the young boys of the City of the Dead, there is only one formal school in the cemetery. Children have to travel long distances to other Cairo districts to attend government schools. Whereas public schooling in Egypt is free, the children of the City of the Dead face the same problems as other members of Cairo's urban poor—schools are overcrowded and underfunded. Many schools have had to resort to conducting two shifts during the school day in order to reduce class sizes. Still, the student-to-teacher ratio sometimes exceeds 70-to-1. In such schools, instruction is replaced by babysitting. As a result, in many schools, only those who can afford private lessons receive a decent education. Such lessons are beyond the means of most families residing in the City of the Dead and combine with other associated school costs (clothing, books, pens, and so forth) to place an unmanageable burden on the family economy. Many parents come to view schooling as an unaffordable luxury.

Given the inadequacies of the Egyptian education system, it is easy to understand how children, especially those from areas such as the City of the Dead, fall through the cracks. Enforcing compulsory education has proven to be difficult. Ministry of Education statistics claim a dropout rate of 15 percent to 20 percent for the first sixteen years of education.

It is also physically difficult for students from the cemeteries to do their homework and to study. They are forced to work in rooms in which numerous other activities are taking place, and the noise from such activities and from other children can be deafening. Also, they may not have enough paper or other school supplies necessary to complete their work.

Many of the people of the City of the Dead have come to distrust the school system when, after years of schooling (and the expenses they entail), children are still largely illiterate. In addition, many parents perceive that, with the present lack of opportunity, secondary school graduates fare little better than drop-outs in the search for jobs. As a result, most of the children in the cemeteries receive no more than a primary school education. To some in the City of the Dead, formal education is irrelevant. Instead, they find that apprenticeships or guidance at home by parents provides more opportunities for their children. As a result, many of the children find themselves contributing to the family economy at a very young age. Most Westerners would call this child labor and condemn such acts. Child labor, however, is clearly a Western concept. In traditional Egyptian society, child labor does not necessarily have the negative connotations that it has in the West. It is an accepted act of survival and is often considered as the best preparation for a child's future.

Many young children in the cemeteries do not attend school. Rather, most help their fathers or other relatives at various jobs or work in the informal economy of the cemeteries. The children who are still in school describe the long distances that they have to travel. Still, most demonstrate a desire to continue. One twelve-year-old boy, now working as a mechanic's assistant, claimed that he missed school and his peers, but he was forced to drop out when his father arranged for his job. He said that he enjoyed school but realized that learning to fix cars was more important for his future. Still, he confessed that his secret desire was to learn to speak English.

Although it is more common for boys to be made apprentices and to work outside the home, girls are often taken out of school in order to learn how to run the household. When deciding whether to leave a girl in school (if the parents are economically able to consider this), parents usually predict how the decision will affect the girl's marriage prospects. If schooling is seen as increasing the chances of arranging a favorable marriage, the girl will remain in school. Otherwise, parents may feel that it is more important for the girl to stay at home and learn how to run a household and successfully fulfill the traditional responsibilities of an Egyptian wife and mother. Recognition of schooling as a means to prepare girls for marriage is a new and growing philosophy among residents of the City of the Dead. Still, traditional views remain strong. One woman of the City of the Dead explains that, in her opinion, women taking nontraditional roles is the cause of many of Egypt's problems. She feels that the time girls spend in school is a waste, and that they study subjects that girls have no business learning about. Others in the City of the Dead view education as helpful in training girls to fulfill their traditional roles, especially in their ability to teach their own children (with an emphasis on teaching sons).

There are people in the City of the Dead with higher education degrees. These people, however, are the exception rather than the norm. Among the people of the City of the Dead who were participants in this study, only one, Ashrof, has finished university studies (see p. 78). Mamdouh Abbass (see p. 84) studied English through The Center for Adult and Continuing Education, a nondegree program at The American University in Cairo. Recognizing the benefits of education, both of these men actively encouraged the younger members of their families to study, and they encouraged relatives to leave their children in school. Given the examples of Mamdouh and Ashrof, it seems clear that education *can* be a means of escaping the City of the Dead. Mamdouh has left the cemeteries and Ashrof has the financial means to do so.

RELIGION

About 90 percent of Egyptians are Sunni Muslim. For many, religion is a total way of life. Residents of the City of the Dead tend to be more traditional in their religious practices than formal Cairenes. Religion is a factor in all decisions and actions. Even when struggling to make ends meet, most people of the cemeteries have remained steadfast in their faith. Some see their struggles as a test of their faith in God. Some believe that suffering in this life will bring great rewards in the afterlife. Others, however, feel as if they have been forgotten by their Creator.

Religion permeates the entire atmosphere of the cemetery. As discussed in Chapter 1, the City of the Dead contains some of the most important monuments and shrines of the Muslim world. At many shrines, annual religious festivals bring people to the City of the Dead from Cairo, the countryside, and even from other Muslim countries in order to celebrate the lives and achievements of Muslim saints.

Such religious festivals are called *mulids*, and they are typically held on the Muslim saint's birthday. Mulids are usually dedicated either to a *wali*, a spiritual leader of a Sufi clan, or to members of the *ahl el-beit*, the family and companions of the Prophet Muhammad. Some of the most popular mulids include those for Sayyida Nafisa, the Imam al-Shafi'i, and Ibn Al Farid, an Arab Sufi poet. Each mulid has its own blend of prayer and ritual, and attracts visitors from not only Cairo, but from all over Egypt and the Muslim world. There is actually a controversy surrounding mulids. Many Muslims believe that the celebration of mulids is an accepted religious ritual. Others say that mulids are *bidaa*, an improper innovation in Islam. Journalist Steve Negus described the scene at the mulid of Ibn Al Farid:

> As Sheikh Yassin begins to sing the courtyard becomes a tossing and turning mass, on occasion forming into neat lines of swaying bodies, at others going

amorphous. Clusters of dancers emit synchronized grunts as they pound the earth. Massive women in black baladi robes grip their scarves between their teeth and mingle obliviously with tall and emancipated falaheen [farmers] and the occasional Westerner out for a cultural experience.[28]

There are also some private, informal mulids in the City of the Dead. Mamdouh Abbass' family holds a mulid in their tomb-home each year. Men and women travel from distant villages where Mamdouh's family has its roots, and they are joined by one of the local village sheiks. These visitors camp out for two or three days in the courtyard of the Abbass family tomb. The space is divided into separate areas for the men and women, and each socialize in their own spheres. The men will chant verses from the Qu'ran led by the sheik. They often appear to lose control, violently swaying their heads back and forth with tears rolling down their cheeks.

Sayyida Nafisa's mosque and mausoleum, a place of visitation and a popular mulid, is also one of the most popular places in Cairo to get married. Locals claim that there are typically around one hundred weddings a week at Sayyida Nafisa, drawing thousands of Cairenes, many who have never entered the cemeteries before. Here, weddings are usually traditional. The women wait outside while the groom and the bride's father agree to the marriage inside (witnessed by the men and the local sheikh). After the hands of the groom and his new father-in-law have been joined in agreement, festive music and soft drinks are enjoyed by both sexes, inside and outside the mosque. This act is the completion of the *kat b'kkitab*, or the fourth stage in the five stages of courtship. The first stage, or *iltifaq*, is the initial agreement between the groom and the bride's guardian. At this time, the bride-price, dowry, and engagement present are specified. At *fatha*, the second stage, certain verses from the Qu'ran are read at the bride's house. The third stage is called *shabka* and is the actual engagement. At this time the bride is usually given presents of gold and there is typically a party at the bride's house. If the family can afford it, the party will be in the street with festive lights, chairs, music, drinks and pastry for guests to enjoy. During the celebration, men and women will congregate in different areas.

After b'ikkitab, *duxla* the final stage, is when the couple starts to live together. At this time another party is held at the bride's house (many poor families will have only one celebration, either an engagement party or a duxla party). Among traditional families, the bride's honor must be proven at this time. Typically, the bridegroom and a few of the bride's female relatives will gather in a room. The groom must break the hymen of his new wife with his forefinger. A blood-stained cloth will be displayed for guests to see as proof of the bride's virginity. Years earlier the bride probably underwent the painful act of female circumcision, which is still widely practiced in Egypt and which prevents the female from experiencing sexual pleasures. Female circumcision became a source of controversy in 1994 when CNN ran a story on the practice, showing the operation being performed on a ten year old Egyptian girl. There is a growing movement to ban the practice.

The City of the Dead is also flooded with visitors from Cairo proper and the countryside during important religious feasts such as Ramadan. During these times, traditional Egyptian families will typically visit their dead. Some families will even live at the tombs for an extended period, especially during the last seven days of Ramadan. For some of the more permanent residents of the cemeteries this can become problematic. They may have to move out and stay in the streets every time the true owners come to visit their departed. During visits, the owners of the tombs may decide that they no longer will allow the squatters to seek shelter in the tombs and will attempt to have them forcibly removed (see Chapter 3, p. 97).

On Thursday evenings and on Fridays, family members of the deceased (mostly women and children) can be seen flocking to the cemeteries to visit and offer prayers to the dead. Usually dressed in traditional black *baladi* robes, women arrive in taxis or on foot, carrying food, portable gas burners, and other offerings for the deceased. They are met at the gates to the City of the Dead by men selling flowers and incense. Frequently the visitors will burn the incense and recite verses from the Qu'ran at the tomb. The women may also prepare food at the grave site and offer flowers.

This visiting and offering to the dead is a continuation of a practice of picnicking with the dead dating back to Pharaonic times.* In those days, the act was meant to provide nourishment to the deceased in order to ensure his or her good health in the afterlife. Dr. Nadia el-Saftey, a professor of sociology at the American University in Cairo claims, "The phenomenon of relatives visiting the dead on Islamic feast days and weekends is a cultural phenomenon and a necessary ritual with evident ties to the legacy of ancient Egypt."[29] This cultural phenomenon is carried out by numerous Egyptians from all strata of society. Former first lady Jehan Sadat wrote about her own visits to the cemeteries with her family.

> Twice a year on our religious feasts and on the birthdays of relatives who had passed away, we went as a family to the City of the Dead, the huge cemetery

---

*This practice was also carried out by the ancient Greeks and Romans and, in more recent times, by some Europeans.

which stretches to the east of Cairo. On the day of the feasts, the road to the cemetery would be jammed with traffic—cars and donkey carts bearing loads of flowers and food. Like many other families, we gave away gifts of food and money to the needy who gathered there, and read verses from the Quran to bring light into even the darkest graves and comfort to the souls of those no longer on earth.[30]

People are also drawn to the cemeteries for reasons less festive than mulids and weddings. Numerous sick and poor Egyptians travel in search of blessings from the dead and alms from the living. Or they will travel to the monuments of highly revered Muslim saints so they can die there. Others will go to ask for blessings or to pray for a favor such as fertility. Even more religious Egyptians from various parts of Egypt will make a vow to visit the holy shrines of the cemeteries at least once before death. It is not uncommon to witness donkey carts arriving at Sayyida Nafisa, or to see another popular shrine filled with *falaheen* who have traveled from the distant countryside to make the pilgrimage. For many, it is their first trip to the city.

RELATIONS WITH FORMAL CAIRENES

Whereas there is significant contact between residents of the City of the Dead and many formal Cairenes, the relationship between the groups is not always genial. Dr. el-Saftey of the American University in Cairo notes that "Occupants of the City of the Dead oftentimes have a negative relationship with formal Cairene society. They are classified as different, as not being the norm. Living with the dead is simply not accepted [in modern Egypt]."[31]

Many Cairenes simply choose to ignore the phenomenon of the living among the dead. Others still are simply unaware of the vast numbers living in the City of the Dead. Some Cairenes consider living with the dead to be *haram*—an activity forbidden by Islam—and condemn the people of the City of the Dead for this activity. These people often fail to recognize, however, that most of the residents of the City of the Dead have few alternatives.

There is considerable discrimination against those who live in the cemeteries. Taxis frequently refuse to take passengers whose destination is one of the cemeteries. Employers may be skeptical about hiring someone who lives in the City of the Dead. Children from the area feel compelled to lie to their schoolmates about where they live to avoid being teased or ostracized.

Unfortunately, many Egyptians will blame the residents of the City of the Dead for creating their own grim circumstances. Residents will be seen as a nuisance to society much the same way that welfare recipients in the United States are often perceived. Some Egyptians have sympathy for the people of the cemeteries but believe that, in society, there are those who are supposed to be in the upper, middle, and lower classes, and those who are condemned to lives of poverty. Egyptian society has very rigid social classes and there is very little social mobility. Egyptians are identified as being a member of a social class and this identification goes a long way in defining who someone is and what opportunities will be given to that person. The concepts of equality of person and of opportunity have little basis in Egypt. Whereas Westerners often preach that everyone is created equal regardless of their economic status, race, or educational background, such theories are foreign to Egyptian society and will remain this way until real democratic initiatives are introduced to Egypt, and the people are given a sense of empowerment.

CRIME AND ISLAMIC MILITANCY

The lack of opportunity and education has caused some of the cemeteries' residents to turn to crime. In fact, there is a long history of crime associated with the people in the City of the Dead. Criminals and runaways have long sought shelter among the tombs where they would not be caught easily. Such a scenario is described in *The Thief and the Dogs*, a popular short story by Nobel Prize-winning author Naguib Mahfouz. In the story, a thief who has hidden in the cemeteries looks across his vast refuge and observes, "What a lot of graves there are, laid out as far as the eye can see. Their headstones are like hands raised in surrender, though they are beyond being threatened by anything. A city of silence and truth, where policemen and thieves lie side by side in peace for the first time."[32] Scenes involving crime and runaways in the cemeteries also frequently occur in Egyptian films, television, and theater.

Still, the cemetery is a relatively safe place aside from the hordes of children who encircle visitors. Many Egyptians, however, will warn people not to go there. With the masses of people making their homes among the tombs of the cemeteries and the frequent visitors to the dead, the City of the Dead is no longer such an attractive hiding place for outlaws. Some sections of the cemeteries do, however, have a valid reputation for drug trafficking and parts of the Northern Cemetery are littered with discarded syringes. Residents point to unemployed neighbors who mysteriously are able to afford Western-style clothing and gold jewelry. Others describe cars entering the cemetery late at night. People appear from behind the tombs to meet the driver, and money and hashish exchange hands.

Today, most of the criminals in the City of the Dead are not runaways or ex-convicts who have gone there to seek shelter. Rather, they are a small number of the residents of the cemeteries who have become disillusioned and have turned to crime as a solution. For a few willing to go to extremes to change their position in society, drugs, theft, prostitution, and religious militancy become attractive alternatives.

Resurgent Islam in Egypt has been a topic of debate since the assassination of President Anwar Sadat in October 1981. The roots of the movement lie in the nationalistic fervor of the early twentieth century and the creation of a paramilitary wing of the Muslim Brotherhood in the 1930s. Militant activities have been stepped up in recent years and have accounted for more than 400 deaths. The government has responded with an unprecedented anti-terrorism campaign.

Areas of informal housing such as the City of the Dead are considered to be potential breeding grounds for extremism, including terrorism and Islamic fundamentalism, because of their harsh living conditions. However, the widely rumored militancy of the City of the Dead has not yet been substantiated. The government fears that if people begin to view secular leadership as having failed them, the appeal of religious leadership increases. Realizing that these slum areas are potential breeding grounds for fundamentalist activity (especially after the December 1992 clash between police and the militant Jamaat Islamiya in the poor Cairo suburb of Imababa), the government has included an urban development program as part of its strategy in confronting militant fundamentalist movements.

Although crime exists in the City of the Dead, the real crime is the fact that people are forced to resort to living among and within tombs. Like many Third World countries, Egypt has been unable to provide a decent quality of life within the formal system for many of its poor. The government has been unable to create jobs for these people who typically fall through the cracks. They have been ostracized from society. Still, they have created their own existence. They have become imaginative in their situations by providing their own housing in an illegal society. They are the victims of an economic and social system, which they view as oppressive. In the face of such a system, they feel that they have no more power to better their situations. Their only hope is that a real change will occur in the Egyptian people, the system and its administration, and that the needs of people like themselves will be positively addressed. In this way, their children can escape the hardships of the only world they have ever known—the society of the dead.

STORIES

I knew that there was a tomb in the cemetery that was special for my family. I had visited on holidays with my mother when I was younger and said goodbye to her at the same place. I also knew that people were increasingly using the cemetery as a place to live. At first, I couldn't imagine living there.

—Mohamed
Resident of the Cemetery of the Great

Like the women of the City of the Dead, men have faced their share of challenges forced to live among the tombs. First and foremost, they are often seen as failures for having to resort to a life in the cemeteries at all. They have failed as fathers and as husbands for not being able to provide a decent standard of living for their families. For most men, such thoughts weigh on their minds day and night.

ASHROF MOHAMED
Sir

Ashrof Mohamed's favorite attire is a Benetton shirt with stylish black designer jeans. To see him, one would hardly expect that he lives in the City of the Dead. Ashrof, however, was born in the cemeteries and has lived there all of his life as one of the City's more atypical residents.

My family comes from a village in the Galayoub district of the Nile Delta region about one hour outside of Cairo. My parents moved to the city after numerous friends of my father, earlier migrants to Cairo, returned to the village and encouraged them to move. They claimed that life in the city had more to offer. My father and mother decided to move to this area because they would be near their friends who had traveled before them. Indeed, there was a growing community of migrants from my father's village. So, he set off to find a better life than the countryside was providing.

Ashrof's parents settled in a building built in the urbanized area near the complex of the Sultan Qaytbay in the Northern Cemetery. Although surrounded by tombs and at the cemetery's heart, their dwelling does not contain a tomb. Here, Ashrof's father worked as a cobbler and shoemaker as he and his wife raised two daughters and three sons.

I guess that I was an unusual child for this area. I was given opportunities, and I took advantage of them. My parents recognized that I was very intelligent from a young age, and they made a lot of sacrifices so that I could get a good education. Sometimes my mother and sisters would go for days with very little food to afford my private lessons. I finished primary, prep, and secondary school and went on to study law at Ain Shams University. This was no small accomplishment. I had to travel long distances to school, and the noise and other conditions of this area made it almost impossible to study. Anyway, I graduated with honors and was given a job working in a Cairo courthouse. Soon, however, I earned a reputation and was able to open up my own law office.

The death of Ashrof's father provided him with new challenges and responsibilities.

After my father died it was up to me to take over the responsibilities of the family business that my father had been trying to build. I think that my legal and business knowledge helped me a great deal as I made some changes and expanded my father's shoe operation. We no longer make the shoes in-house. Instead, we now buy them wholesale from a company in the Nasr City suburb of Cairo and re-sell them here for a small profit. We converted the ground floor of our home into a small shop and added large display windows. Now, most of our living quarters are upstairs.

The shoe business has actually proven to be more profitable than my law practice, and I find myself spending most of my time here taking care of the daily operations of the shop and traveling back and forth by motorcycle to Nasr City to pick up new shipments of shoes. I am especially busy during feasts and holidays such as Ramadan as the traditional residents of the area will save their money and will sometimes borrow money in order to buy the children new shoes. The same will happen at the beginning of the school year. During these times the shop usually stays open until one o'clock in the morning.

Our life is fairly comfortable compared to most people who live in the surrounding area. We have electricity, running water, as well as one of the few private phones in the area. Most of the people here have to use government-installed public telephones near the Mosque of Sultan Barquq. Many people also do not have running water and have to rely on the public tap beside Qaytbay Mosque.

In addition to his cemetery residence and law office, Ashrof owns a small apartment in Nasr City, which he rents out for an additional source of income. He is also engaged to be married, a luxury many men of the City of the Dead cannot afford. His fiancee, like him, lives in the Northern Cemetery with her family. Upon their marriage, the couple plans to live together in the cemetery with Ashrof's family.

Ashrof is highly regarded and respected for his accomplishments by other members of the community around the Qaytbay complex. In the evening, he typically walks to a local coffee house to play cards and smoke a waterpipe. He will be greeted with warmth and admiration by the other patrons, and the owner of the shop will reserve the best chair for him. It is not uncommon for men twice his age to address him as Sir Ashrof. Ashrof also seems to realize his own importance. He enjoys talking at length about himself, his accomplishments, and most importantly, the many women he says are in love with him.

Setting himself apart from the cemetery, Ashrof talks about its inhabitants with disapproval. Even though his home is in the very heart of the Northern Cemetery and is surrounded by tombs, Ashrof insists he doesn't live in the cemetery. He has convinced himself that because his home is not built above a tomb, he should not be counted among the tomb-dwellers of the City of the Dead. Perhaps his exalted status is what keeps him residing in the cemetery. Outside of the City of the Dead he might merely be another Cairo resident.

Outsiders should be careful when visiting the cemetery and should never come after dark. The area is very dangerous, especially for foreigners. Most of the problems are a result of a lack of education among the youth. Most of the children here attend only primary school. Many of them, if not most, are illiterate and can only write their names. With such little education and so few opportunities, many of the teenagers turn to drugs and crime as an avenue to try to better their lives. The cemetery is a major market in Cairo for heroin and hashish. Look at that four-story building built above a tomb. Where do you think that the money comes from?

Most of the people of the cemetery do not look like normal city dwellers, and they don't think like them either. Residents of the city normally have good knowledge of penalties for crimes. A majority of the people who live here in the City of the Dead, however, are migrants from the countryside who come from areas where there are few rules and even less enforcement. An outsider has to be careful when dealing with these people. If they would like to make a problem with you, they are not going to take time to think about the possible consequences. They act before they think. Their hands are quicker than their minds.

I remember some time ago there was a wife of some ambassador to Egypt who wanted to see the situation of the people living in the cemetery first-hand. I guess that she wanted to help the poor. She left her nice diplomatic Mercedes near one of the cemetery's gates and set out to investigate. Of course, when she returned she found all of the windows smashed and everything taken out from inside. Anyway, she was lucky that that was all that happened.

Like many of the residents of the City of the Dead, Ashrof has heard rumors of government plans to move the tombs and their inhabitants to places outside of Cairo and to redevelop the area currently occupied by the City of the Dead.

I support the plan enthusiastically. The area would be much better if it contained modern apartment buildings and gardens.

Of course, with another apartment in Nasr City, Ashrof has fewer worries about his family's future than most. He holds an idealistic view of the government's ability to accommodate those thousands upon thousands of poorer residents who might be rendered homeless by providing affordable housing elsewhere, a view held by few others in the City of the Dead.

ARABE
His Generation

Like Ashrof, Arabe's roots are in the Galayoub district of Egypt. Unlike Ashrof, however, his life has followed a more traditional route of migrants from the countryside: one of struggle, indigence, and dissatisfaction with urban life.

My grandfather left the fields and his familiar surroundings to come here to Cairo based on the advice of friends who had already made the move. I don't know if he ever decided deep down inside whether it was a good decision or not but, like his friends, he never would have admitted that it was a bad one. He was an ambitious man, and he moved his family because he saw the move to the city as his only hope for obtaining a truly fulfilling life. I guess he was desperate for change and eager to better himself and to provide more for his family. He hoped to achieve his dreams of financial and material comfort or at least to give his children the opportunity to achieve these goals.

When he finally came to Cairo, I don't think he found the city he expected after listening to his friends' stories. They had aggrandized it so that it seemed so inviting. Instead, he found an urban environment that is unfriendly to newcomers and to its poor.

He came to settle in the Northern Cemetery by following his friends' examples. At that time, the area was just beginning to become a popular refuge for migrants and other poor from the city. Of course, he was only supposed to live in the cemetery temporarily. Here, he set out to find the better life he sought.

My grandfather soon discovered that his qualifications could fetch him only the most menial, low-paying jobs in Cairo. Instead of accepting such a position, he decided to look inward to the growing community he had suddenly become a part of. With what little money he had managed to save before moving, he bought the ingredients to prepare fried potatoes, *tamia* [a mixture of ground beans, coriander, garlic and other spices which are formed into balls and deep fried] *and foul* [fava beans], *and he began selling his wares from a push cart that he had made and pushed through the streets of the cemetery. Such traditional foods, staples in the diet of Egypt's poor, are inexpensive to prepare (which was ideal to his needs) and are inexpensive to purchase (which was ideal for the customers in the cemetery).

When my grandfather first moved here the cemetery was quite different. It wasn't as developed as it is today. People had been and were continuing to live in only the one-story structures built around the family tomb plots. As the years passed, however, it became evident to my grandfather and to the many others that their tombs would be their permanent homes. When they realized that, they began to save and invest their money to make these structures more livable, more like the homes they had left. This led to the overcrowding and expansion of the most populated parts of the cemetery. Now you can see three and four story buildings in some places.

My grandfather used this same idea with his business. He invested in his food service. His push cart became a permanent stand on the roadside, and soon after there was a small room he built to store supplies. His son, my father, worked alongside him as a young boy and eventually inherited the task of running the business and the household when my grandfather died.

I guess this is where I come into the story. I was born here, in the cemetery, as Sayed Mohamed al-Agouz, but everyone came to call me simply Arabe. The tomb-dwelling, family business, and dreams of a better life and of *leaving this awful place have all been passed down to me, the third generation of my family to live in the cemetery.*

I worked as a food vendor with my father since the early days of my childhood, and now I do it alone. I guess I inherited the major responsibilities of running the kiosk when I completed preparatory school. That was more education than anyone else in my family had ever received, and my father thought that it was enough. My father still oversees things; that is he spends his day sitting beside the food stand, watching and talking with the people and looking at the newspaper (although he really can't read).

Sitting side by side, the father appears as if he is waiting to die while the son is waiting to live. Arabe talks with pride about the profession he has inherited. He looks fondly at the food stand and explains how it was nothing more than a make-shift structure until his father remodeled it in 1944 to its present shape. The lime green paint is a more recent addition.

When business is slow, Arabe can be seen gazing aimlessly across the rooftops of the tomb-homes. His imagination wanders, bringing him to another time and another place far away from the poverty within the cemeteries' borders. He imagines he is living and working in another area.

Any area is better than this one. I know I am better off than some people who live in the cemetery, whose lives are absolutely desolate. I thank God for that. Still, I dream of having a real apartment and a restaurant downtown. I dream of large windows looking out into the street inviting all of the passers by to try my food. Also, there would have to be a large aluminum door where all of the customers would enter, as well as a lot of decoration. It would be a big change from this kiosk where I have to stand in the street all day under the sun.

I would like to make some improvements to my kiosk but that would be self-defeating. If the people of the cemetery see a shop with nice decoration and which looks respectable, they would be afraid to eat there thinking that the food will be expensive and unaffordable for them. I must confess myself, when I leave the cemetery and go to other areas of the city and I see all of the clean shops with their fluorescent signs and nice tables and chairs, I hesitate before entering. I am embarrassed to have to ask the price of anything before I order it. I guess I feel this way because my education has been life in the cemetery. I know how people here think and we think like this. Most of us are uneducated and without money. We have never had anything nice. We know what the majority of society thinks of us, and we are embarrassed and ashamed.

I had hoped to achieve my grandfather's dream by moving out of the cemetery before I started a family of my own, but time was not on my side. My father, old and tired, asked me last year to hurry and marry because he wanted to see his only son settled and with children before he died. What could I do? I carried out his wishes of course, and I married a young woman who is also from the cemetery. We live together with my parents, and my wife is now expecting a child.

He says this with both anticipation and remorse. Another mouth to feed means less money saved. Less money saved pushes the goal of moving out of the cemetery farther and farther away. Arabe worries about saving money.

What if I fall seriously ill? If I didn't work for one week there would be no more money left to support my family.

For now, Arabe will stand at the kiosk from seven in the morning until two in the afternoon, forming balls of tamia and dropping them into the sizzling grease. The shirt proclaiming "INTERNATIONAL" and the pajama bottoms he wears to work everyday will continue to accumulate years of grease. His evenings will be spent in a cemetery coffee house fretting and fantasizing about life along with the other men, young and old, who find themselves trapped in the City of the Dead. It seems that for Arabe's family, the realization of lifetimes of dreams will have to wait at least one more generation.

MAMDOUH ABBASS
My First and True Home

Mamdouh Abbass' family tomb is on the edge of the Southern Cemetery close to where Salah Salem Highway passes between the cemetery and the Citadel. It is a fairly large tomb complex containing four rooms and a courtyard. It is superior to much of the housing in other poor or slum areas of Greater Cairo. One room is used for multi-purposes such as sitting, eating, and sleeping. This room is about six feet wide by eight feet long. The floor is cement with a plastic carpet covering it. The walls are painted blue and decorated with a few old family photographs and a wall clock in the shape of a silver wrist watch. There are two small windows, one on each side of the room, covered over with steel bars. The only furniture is three hand crafted wooden benches covered with stuffed cushions. Wire strung across the wall and across the tombs outside provides life to an ancient television set that is always on.

Another room is a small kitchen. This room is no more than three feet wide and five feet long. There is barely enough room to turn around in the space into which a refrigerator and gas stove are stuffed. A water tap drips constantly, and assorted dishes and pans are scattered around. There is little storage space for food. Still, poor Egyptian families usually buy what they need on a day-to-day or every other day basis.

A bathroom is partitioned off to the side. The room is no bigger than a cupboard and you must lean your body over the ceramic toilet in order to close the door. The Abbass family is fortunate to have a ceramic toilet (although it does not flush), however, and not a latrine (or nothing at all) like most households of the City of the Dead.

The third room is Mamdouh's parents' bedroom, a six foot square room that is filled from wall to wall by their bed. The final room is almost completely filled with a tombstone. The room is about the same size as the bedroom. The tombstone, two feet across and five feet long, protrudes from the ground some four feet high. It is made of cement and painted blue with a white top. At one end, a stela rises another two feet into the air. Some books and an iron sit on top of the tomb and clothes hang on nails protruding from the walls of the room. Unlike most of the tombs of the Southern Cemetery, the Abbass family has running water and electricity.* They do not, however, have a telephone, and must cross Salah Salem Highway to reach the nearest public phone.

Behind the living quarters is an enclosed courtyard. A lone palm tree provides shade, and a group of ducks wander beneath its branches. The courtyard is bricked with the exception of a rectangular area near the center. Here is the door leading to the underground chambers where most of Mamdouh's family is buried.

Under the howsh [courtyard] *is the tombs of my family. They can be entered where the dirt patch is. If you remove the dirt, you will find two stone slabs which can be dislodged. After they are removed, a cement staircase which leads down to the tombs is revealed. There is a tomb for the men on the left and a tomb for the women of my family on the right. We are kept separate in death as it would be haram* [sinful] *for us to be buried together. The tomb is opened every time someone from my family dies. That person is returned to God along with his other relatives. Only my godfather has his own tomb, which is under the room with his tombstone. This tomb is special*

---

*I was never sure if the electricity in the Abbass household was received legally or if they had tapped into local wires. I assume that it was acquired legally as the government had installed running water in the area.

for him because he was much loved by everyone in my family. This tomb is closed and cannot be entered again.

My family is very close-knit. I have lived all of my life in Cairo, but my ancestors come from the countryside near Zagazig. Many relatives still live there and will come once a year to this tomb when we have a small mulid [religious festival] *in honor of the dead. This is a time for my family to come together and visit as well as to honor our dead. It is a very exciting time, and the tomb is filled with distant relatives from the countryside. There is hardly a place to sit. Everybody takes part in the activities. The women socialize and prepare food and drinks for the men. The children play games outside. They clap and dance and make so much noise! The men catch up on all the news there is to report and engage in prayer. A sheik comes from the countryside and reads from the Qu'ran. His words become like magic.*

Mamdouh explains how they came to live in the cemetery:

My father has a shop for aluminum items such as trays, bowls, pots and pans in the square at the base of the Citadel. We used to live in an apartment above the shop when I was a child. When we lived there we would always come and visit the family tomb at feasts and would stay there sometimes for days or weeks, especially at the end of Ramadan. My father was very close to his godfather when he was alive. Now, he is buried in the tomb, and my father likes to visit him and be near him. After spending so much time at the tomb, we finally moved here seven years ago. Since most of my brothers and sisters were already grown and married, for most of the time it has been only myself, my parents, my brother Said, and my sister Azza who has lived here.*

Said and Azza are both younger than Mamdouh. Said is tall, thin and shy—especially with women. If a young woman walks into the room, his chin will drop and his face will become red. Azza is heavy-set, of medium height, and has a baby face. She wears traditional Egyptian dress of galabeya and headscarf, and she seldom leaves the house except to visit relatives. Even then, she is usually escorted by one of her brothers, a nephew, or cousin. Over the course of two years, Azza changed a great deal. At first, she seemed young and immature. She soon was engaged to be married, however, and began to take her responsibilities more seriously. Her family

---

*I have seen the apartment above Mamdouh's father's shop where they used to live. No one has lived there since they moved out, and it looks uninhabitable. I think that the choice to move was not as voluntary as Mamdouh suggested. The old apartment was probably on the verge of being condemned, and the move was more practical than elective.

always teased her that she would not make a good housewife, which made her try harder to succeed. She was married and left the City of the Dead to live with her new husband in Basateen, another poor area of informal housing in Cairo.

Now only Said is left with his parents as both Mamdouh and Azza have gotten married and moved out of the cemetery. Mamdouh's family is very traditional. His mother is an elderly woman who looks all of her sixty plus years. Still, she is quite active and can usually be found in the home taking care of the household tasks and entertaining a number of ever-present family visitors. Old age is beginning to catch up with her, as she is frequently sick. Sometimes she has to spend days in bed, and the different medicines that she has to take are a drain on the Abbass family's limited resources. Still, she always has a smile on her face and only kind words to say.

Like his mother, Mamdouh's father is also showing his advanced years. He is of medium height, has white hair, and is frail. Still, he works six days a week selling aluminum in his shop. He'll come home at the end of the day with a bag of bread or fruit in his hand. He removes the outer layers of his clothing, sits and rests. A few minutes later he is off to wash and to prepare for praying. Typically he prays in the room filled with the grave marker of his godfather. He is a very religious man who is almost never seen without his prayer beads, which he busily rubs between his fingers. He often falls into deep religious contemplation and calls out the name of God at random. *Allah!* He is a very quiet man who seldom raises his voice. Like his wife, he is an optimist, always trying to see the good in everything and everyone.

Mealtime is a family event. When the family sits down to eat, the women will serve the food on a large aluminum tray set on the floor. The family will sit around the tray and eat. If only the immediate family is present, they will all sit and eat together. If there are guests, however, the men will frequently be served first with the women eating after the men have finished, often taking their meal in the courtyard. The meal is conducted in a manner traditionally Egyptian. No one has their own plate. The different types of food are displayed in common bowls from which all partake. If there is chicken or meat, portions are usually divided up by Mamdouh's mother and passed to each person wrapped in a piece of bread. When I first became friends with Mamdouh, I was treated as a guest. At mealtimes, I was always given the largest portions of meat or chicken. I was given utensils to eat with while others ate with their hands. Cushions were placed under me while others sat directly on the floor. I was grateful when the day came that I was no longer treated as a guest, and the family no longer felt that they had to go out of their way to ensure my comfort.

Mamdouh is very close to his family. His love and admiration for his parents are evident in his constant care for them. He can remember only one time when any serious problems invaded their relationship.

Many years ago, my father took a second wife. She was his cousin and was more beautiful, more worldly, and more educated than my mother. I don't know how he got himself into this situation exactly. I guess that he just couldn't resist her at the time. He wanted to have sex with her but knew that he couldn't unless they were married. So, he married her and they even had two children together. Throughout all of this, none of us knew about my father's secret wife.

My mother found out years later. Of course, she was furious at having been deceived by the man she loved. All of the family was furious. Can you imagine being married and finding out that your spouse has been married to another person at the same time? Can you imagine finding out that your father had another wife that you didn't know about? Well, my mother moved out and returned to live with her family. When my father went to ask about her to try to make peace, my grandfather told him that he had to make a choice. He had to choose one of his wives, either my mother or his second wife. He could not have both but must divorce one. In the end, my father chose love over sex and divorced his second wife. My mother returned to him and they have been fairly happy ever since.

Of course after this happened it was difficult for my mother to forget quickly about the problem and to completely put it behind her, especially because she would frequently see this other woman (because she was part of the family). When they would meet, they did not want to be in the same room together, and they refused to try to get along. Still, our families tried to get them to reconcile their differences. Then, one of the sons my father had fathered with the other woman suddenly died shortly after he finished his university studies. We buried him here in the family tomb. In this way, his mother would have to come and mourn here five days a week. She and my mother were forced to stay together in the same house and reconcile their differences. It worked! Amazingly enough, they are actually good friends today. This other woman comes to visit my mother and they sit and talk for hours. Now that they are older, the jealousy between them has died.

Reconciliation is a family affair. Even when Azza began having problems with her husband, the two were not expected to work out their difficulties by themselves. Instead, a family gathering was called in the Abbass family tomb-home. Both Azza and her husband were given a chance to explain their differences and a family discussion ensued. The participants then came

The Modern Era

to a conclusion on how to rectify the situation, which both Azza and her husband were compelled to abide.

Mamdouh never demonstrated any shame about his life in the cemetery. He recognized the burdens of life in the City of the Dead but always carried himself with pride. When we set off for the cemetery to hold his English lessons, we would have to take a crowded city bus. Taxi drivers would refuse to take us. Still, Mamdouh never got discouraged. Even the first time that Mamdouh brought me to his home, he did not act embarrassed or ashamed. Both he and his family welcomed me warmly. His family came to treat me as one of their own and gave me an adopted name, Ismail Abbass. Although they could not speak any English, and my Arabic was still in its elementary stages, we would find ways of communicating with each other. Even without verbal communication, the mutual love and respect between myself and Mamdouh's family was easily felt.

Mamdouh worked in a private office downtown, which buys items at auction prices and re-sells them. He made LE 150–200 per month. Most of the day, he would sit and try to make sense of countless papers with government stamps on them. He never enjoyed his work but always felt fortunate for the work that he had. When he began working in this office he was living with his family and didn't have many expenses. He saved money for when he would get married. His first marriage, however, was brief and ended sourly. He had married a young girl from an area neighboring the cemetery.

She was beautiful and I thought that we were in love. I quickly learned, however, that she was not a good person. I really misjudged her. When we got married we lived in the cemetery with my parents. There is only one bedroom, and that is occupied by my parents. In the summer we could sleep in the courtyard, but in the winter we had to crowd into the living room along with my sister and brother. We had no privacy. I wanted to get an apartment for the two of us elsewhere, but it was too difficult at that time. This didn't satisfy her. She hated living in the cemetery and claimed that she wanted us to have our own apartment in a more acceptable area. She began to want everything except me. We began to fight a lot, and I suspected that she liked other men and was flirting with them. I divorced her and rid myself of that situation.

After his failed marriage, Mamdouh began to save his money for other purposes. He started to take English classes at the American University in Cairo's night school, and I would tutor him in his home. Little did he know what a profound effect these classes would have on his life. On the last day of one of his courses in the spring of 1993, Mamdouh asked me to attend with him. Something unexpected was happening. After handing out final grades, Sandy, the Canadian teacher, had an announcement to make. She was planning a wedding with one of her students. It was Mamdouh. They had known each other for only two months but had somehow fallen in love and decided to take a leap into marriage. While the other students in the class stared in disbelief, Mamdouh looked as happy as a child on Christmas morning. Even I, one of his closest friends, had no idea of any connection between Sandy and Mamdouh beyond an academic one.

Mamdouh was nervous because until this time he had not informed Sandy of where he lived or of how little his monthly salary was. While having dinner in a restaurant that night after the class these subjects came up in conversation. Sandy was surprised but not discouraged. The wedding was still on.

The engagement party was held in the courtyard of the tomb-home in the cemetery. There was pastry, Arabic music, dancing, and lots of smiling. It was a joyous occasion. For most of Mamdouh's family, Sandy represented a world that was quite foreign to them. The closest they had been to foreigners was watching them in American and British television programs. Dressed in jeans with her long, dirty-blond hair falling to the side and smoking a cigarette, Sandy was not the typical woman seen in the City of the Dead. Still, the Abbass family accepted her with open hearts, open minds, and a great deal of curiosity. Sandy would sit in the Abbass family tomb-home while Mamdouh's family and friends questioned her time and time again about her ambitions to marry. They made sure that she realized the Islamic expectations of a good wife as well as their own expectations. She assured them that she would do her best to make Mamdouh happy. Sandy's friends and colleagues also questioned her at length about the marriage. Most of them advised her against marrying an Egyptian man, especially one from the cemetery. Soon, however, Mamdouh and Sandy were man and wife.

Marriage is not always easy, and this young marriage was not without its problems. Many of Sandy and Mamdouh's problems were related to housing. Prior to their marriage, Sandy was living in a decent furnished apartment, in the upper-class Cairo suburb of Mohandaseen. Her job at the American University in Cairo paid about ten times the salary that Mamdouh's job paid. It is uncommon in Egypt for a wife to make more than her husband (unless she is the only one working), and this was a difficult situation for Mamdouh to accept. He did not want to move into the Mohandaseen apartment which cost three times his monthly salary. Yet, he wouldn't dream of having Sandy move into the cemetery with his family. He had to solve the question of where they could live.

There was an empty apartment in Basateen, an area of informal housing on the far outskirts of Cairo, which was owned by a relative of Mamdouh. He knew that he and Sandy could live there virtually rent-free. In this way, he wouldn't be in a situation where he was living in an apartment his wife was paying for. Also, it was in a building in which one of his sisters and her family lived allowing them to be near his family, something that was important to him. When he suggested the idea of moving to Basateen to Sandy and she agreed, she had little idea how difficult life would be there.

The walls were painted, a hot water heater was installed, and furniture was brought into the apartment. Still, no paint could cover up the miseries of Basateen. Garbage piled up in the streets around pools of sewage. Nearby factories filled the air with thick black smoke and noise. Most of the housing is self-assembled, and buildings appear to be falling down on top of each other. The commute there from downtown, where Sandy and Mamdouh worked, required that they battle physically to get onto one of a number of minibuses that run on erratic schedules. Sometimes three or four buses and a lot of pushing and shoving would pass before Sandy was able to get a seat. There was little choice. Few taxis could be commissioned to go to such an area as Basateen.

For many, if not most, of the residents of Basateen, Sandy was the first Westerner that they had ever seen. No one could imagine that a foreigner was living there. Soon, Sandy couldn't believe it herself. She became depressed and angry with the living situation. This caused strain in the marriage. She was so frustrated that she virtually stopped doing any kind of household activities in rebellion. Fights became recurrent. Mamdouh began spending more and more time with his family back in the cemetery. Still, he did not reveal his marital problems to them because he did not want to tarnish their favorable opinions of his new wife. Secretly, however, he talked to friends about the possibility of divorce (if things didn't improve). He was also frustrated because Sandy had not yet become pregnant, and he was eager to have children.

It became apparent that the only solution was to move out of Basateen. Mamdouh was able to find a fairly inexpensive apartment in the downtown area of Bab al-Louk. To Sandy, it was like a palace after the horrors of Basateen. For both of them, work was in walking distance, an added bonus. No more crowded buses. Here, Sandy's smile and former personality returned, especially with the news that she was a mother-to-be.

Mamdouh and Sandy later moved to the affluent Cairo suburb of Mohandaseen. Sandy taught English at a prestigious language institute and Mamdouh kept working at his old job. Both of them were waiting excitedly for Mamdouh's visa application to be processed so that they could travel to Canada and show Sandy's relatives their beautiful daughter Jasmine. Finally, the visa arrived and Mamdouh set off with his young family for Canada where they are living together happily. In doing so, Mamdouh completed an amazing journey from the cemeteries of the City of the Dead across the Atlantic to his new home in Canada. He may be the only person from the City of the Dead to have accomplished such a feat. In any case, he is not your typical resident of the City of the Dead.

Mamdouh expressed anxiety and excitement about traveling, but he knows he could never stay away from Egypt and his family for too long.

I still miss living with my family. Their home is in the cemetery and that will always be my first home, the home that I will always come back to. I have never truly felt at home any place else.

MOHAMED
Life, Politics and Sophia Loren

Off to the side of Sayyida Nafisa Mosque in the Cemetery of the Great is a small tomb that is covered with flowering plants. The surrounding tombstones are covered with drying laundry. From the tomb's doorway there is a picturesque view of the Citadel rising out of the ground beyond the cemetery. The tomb looks quite festive despite an atmosphere of gloom. Here, life is flourishing among the dead. Inside this oasis of greens and yellows lives Mohamed, a friendly gentleman who is ready to greet visitors, share a cup of tea, and give them an ear-full of his opinions on life, politics, and even the world of sports and entertainment. He has an opinion on every subject and he has all of the time in the world to express them.

Talking is my specialty. I love to talk. People tell me I talk too much and about too many things, but God gave me this mouth. I might as well use it!

My family came here from a village near Zagazig [a city in the Nile Delta region north of Cairo]. *My grandfather had made quite a reputation for himself in that area as a skilled craftsman. He used to do woodworking and finish off apartments as well as doing remodeling. It is the same work my father did and which I eventually inherited.*

My grandfather decided to try his luck in Cairo and soon made a reputation for himself here as well. He taught my father the trade, and soon my father had even exceeded my grandfather's abilities. After some time, my father was working for only the most important people in Cairo, pashas and the elite of society. This was when I was born.

We lived in Abdeen when I was a child. Then, it was a beautiful area of Cairo, not like today. We were well off and living in an area where most of the people were members of the upper class. Here, I learned my father's and my grandfather's trade and began my working life. Soon I was married and had a family of my own. Of course this was all before the 1952 Revolution when life was good, much better than it is nowadays. I loved King Farouk. He was a great man. When the revolution occurred, everything was destroyed. All of the buildings in my area were destroyed, including my house. I went from the upper class to having no place to go. The new government that had caused our destruction claimed we would receive new housing. I never believed them. In fact, they didn't like us. We represented the days before the revolution. They wanted us to suffer and never intended to give us anything.

My brother invited us to live with his family in Giza. We tried it, but I didn't like living with them. I was uncomfortable because it really wasn't my house. I felt like I was imposing. We stayed there for two months before I made the decision that we should leave. I knew that there was a tomb in the cemetery that was special for my family. I had visited it on holidays with my mother when I was younger, and I had said goodbye to her at the same place. I also knew that people were increasingly using the cemetery as a place to live. At first, I couldn't imagine living here. I debated the idea over in my head time and time again. My wife was completely against the idea but I finally made the decision to move, and she reluctantly agreed. We lived in the cemetery for two months, but my wife was not comfortable. We went back to my brother's house. That lasted only forty days before I moved us back to the cemetery again. That was forty years ago, and I haven't moved since.

Here, we raised a family and made the best we could of our lives. It was difficult because the tomb is so small, but we made it work somehow. Now it is only me left here and, although it is still small for even one person, it feels huge and empty to me. Of course, in one sense my wife is still here with me. She died ten years ago and is buried right here alongside my parents, an uncle, a cousin, and a brother.

We had four sons together: Hamdi, Mohsen, Adel, and Atef. Adel is a taxi driver and lives in the cemetery but not in a tomb. Mohsen and Adel make *beautiful Islamic calligraphy on cloth, which they sell in Saudi Arabia. Hamdi is married to a Saudi Arabian girl. They are all great boys. Atef, however, is another story. He could never stand living in the cemetery. He was always rebellious as well. As soon as he finished high school, he left home and never returned. That was ten years ago. I think that the woman who lives next to me gave him the evil eye and caused this to happen. She only had one son and we had four. Of course she was jealous!*

We also had three daughters. They are all married now and have families of their own. They take turns coming here one day a week to do my cooking, cleaning, and washing. It is the one time in the week that I get to eat meat. Actually, I see one of my daughters quite often now because she lives at Moquattam, which is not far away. She moved there after her house in Giza fell down during the earthquake.

Mohamed's tomb-home consists of only one room which, has been partitioned to serve multi-purposes. The living room is the size of a modest walk-in closet. There is a chair, a small table with a color television (his pride and joy), and a tombstone, which is cluttered with newspapers and other assorted items. There is also a small refrigerator. Pictures of his family decorate the walls.

A sheet hangs from the ceiling to separate the living room from the bedroom. There is one small bed. When he sleeps, Mohamed has to curl himself up in order to fit within the bed's surface. There is electricity in the house, but there is no water and no telephone. Water must be fetched from a tap at Sayyida Nafisa Mosque, and he must use the community telephone at the coffee house nearby.

This area is not so bad. Of course I don't want to live here, but where am I going to go? To a satellite city of Cairo? I'd rather live here than out in the middle of the desert. I guess I've grown used to the cemetery over the years. I used to complain a lot. Of course I was used to a totally different standard of life. I lost my extravagant tastes long ago! Actually, there are a lot of famous people buried here. Sophia Loren even came here once to take pictures.

Not all of the people are good. Nowadays, I have to worry about crime and to be careful about who I trust. Two years ago my tomb was robbed during the religious festival at Sayyida Nafisa. The thieves stole a cassette recorder, my clothes (they even took the hangers), and a television. I went to the police but they ignored me. They didn't care.

The same night I was robbed, the sister of one of the government ministers was also robbed while she was at the mulid. Of course there were three police stations investigating her case!

This is how the government of this country works these days. The rich and the powerful get everything, and they ignore and laugh at the poor. Mubarak is not good in my opinion. He cares about showing off to all of the countries of the world and doesn't care about his own. He is always traveling here and there and getting his picture taken. He should come and visit the cemetery. He doesn't care about poor people as long as they are not a serious threat to him. If we tell him that food is expensive he will say don't eat. We need someone like Clinton here in Egypt.

Egypt is beautiful and would be a wonderful country if it had the right leadership. People from all over the world already come to visit us because we are so rich with history. Unfortunately, most of them don't see the real Egypt. They visit the Hilton and the Sheraton and get whisked from monument to monument in luxury air-conditioned buses. No, the real Egypt is here, in the cemetery, in Hussein, in Sayyida Aisha, in the countryside, the places where people are still living according to true Egyptian tradition.

Egypt is a better place to visit than some place like Israel, for example. If you are going to go to Israel you should go to a country like Italy instead. It is much better there. Look at all of the problems between the Israelis and the Palestinians. It's a horrible place. Of course, America loves Israel. They give Israel so much money every year so that it can continue its fight against the Palestinians. I know that not all of Americans think like this, but there are a lot of Jews in America who have a lot of money. Their money buys them power. Sure, the Jews had the problem with Germany. That was horrible. But why did they do the same thing to the Palestinians?

Sudan is another awful place. There is no food there. The Sudanese are all trying to come to Egypt. There are already five million of them in Cairo and most of them are not good people.

Ahhh . . . there are so many problems in the world. Another bomb in London. I guess I should be thankful. All of this talk makes my problems seem real small.

3

THE FUTURE OF THE CITY OF THE DEAD

> The City of the Dead has to be removed from the living heart of our capital.
>
> —Omar Abdel Akher
> Governor of Cairo

The history of the City of the Dead, from its beginnings as a few isolated tombs in the desert to its present-day form as a sprawling refuge for the urban poor, has been recorded in the preceding pages. The future of the necropolises, however, is uncertain. From art historians to Islamic scholars, from government officials to the residents of the City of the Dead, observers have many different views of the future of the cemeteries. It appears, however, that whatever opinion prevails, there will be change ahead for the City of the Dead and its residents. The City has already been witness to centuries of change but perhaps the most important change is yet to come.

GOVERNMENT PLANS

Many reforms have taken place in Cairo since Omar Abdel Akher became Governor in 1991.* Most of the changes have been applauded by Egyptians

---

*Omar Abdel Akher was the Governor of Cairo for six years (1991–1997). In the summer of 1997, President Hosni Mubarak named Abdel-Rehim Shehata Governor of Cairo. Governor Shehata is expected to continue to follow the policies on limiting and redirecting Cairo's expansion as espoused by former Governor Akher.

and foreigners alike. One issue he proposes to address, however, promises to be explosive—the status of the City of the Dead.

"The City of the Dead has to be removed from the living heart of our capital,"[33] Akher said in a newspaper interview. The government plans to move the mortal remains of much of the cemeteries into the desert, outside of the city limits on the Cairo-Suez Road. Then, the City of the Dead will be demolished to reclaim the land it is built upon to be used for new business and tourism projects. Governor Akher insists that both the families and the individuals who live in the City of the Dead, as well as the families who have tombs in the cemeteries, will be compensated and assisted by the government.

He refers to ancient Egypt to justify his plans. He notes that the forefathers of modern Egypt were better planners than their modern-day counterparts, in that they lived on one side of the Nile and buried their dead on the opposite side. "We will copy their example by making new cemeteries for the capital's residents in our desert Cairo-Suez Road,"[34] he states. Still, he recognizes that some people will protest the cemeteries' removal.

Governor Akher also defends the government's proposal as one that will help the residents of the City of the Dead. "Children saw the light in these cemeteries and grew with the sound of wailing and tears. It is inhuman and every Egyptian should be ashamed for allowing their misery to continue,"[35] he says.

The project is moving ahead, and plans for the demolition of the Bab al-Nasr Cemetery are already in place. The plans to remove the cemeteries are part of a larger project to limit and redirect Cairo's expansion. This scheme involves making progress in three areas:

1. The construction of a 95 kilometer Ring Road around Cairo.
2. The creation of new communities in the desert outside of the Ring Road (a total of ten new suburbs is planned).
3. The re-organization of parts of Cairo (including the cemetery areas).

The reorganization plan emphasizes areas of informal housing. President Mubarak recently allocated LE 4 billion to be spent over four years to upgrade or destroy certain informal areas. This was largely a response to the perception that such areas are strongholds of Islamic fundamentalism.

Attempts have been made to identify the residents of the Bab al-Nasr Cemetery and to register all of the tombs on official planning records. Plans call for the street separating the cemetery from the ancient Fatimid gate (also called Bab al-Nasr) to be widened creating a broad thoroughfare stretching from Bab al Sharia Square to Salah Salem Highway. The population of the cemetery will be relocated to the new communities to be

The Future

constructed outside of Cairo. Upper and middle class housing, public parks, and a new luxury hotel are to take the place of the cemetery. Stories about the upcoming removal, destruction, and redevelopment of the area have appeared in the Egyptian government-controlled media. It would appear that the government is testing people's reactions in an attempt to estimate how much opposition will be voiced.

The government's current plan is actually not new but something that it has considered and desired for years. In fact, Janet Abu-Lughod recognized the value that the government sees in reclaiming the land occupied by the City of the Dead as early on as the late 1960s. She wrote in 1971, "The future of the city [City of the Dead] is moot. Cairo's planners eye the district covetously but in secret, for here is a logical direction into which the cramped city might expand, if only the tombs could be removed!"[36] Abu-Lughod also recognized that there would be significant protest to any plan to remove the tombs of the cemeteries. She writes, "But the sheer size of the zone and the permanence of many of the tomb structures, as well as their high artistic merits, defy simple clearance, even if the revulsion against disturbing the dead could be overcome."[37]

THE CITIZENS' RESPONSE

The main opposition to the project will probably come from three groups: the residents of the City of the Dead, tomb owners, and historians of art and of Islam and other scholars who appreciate the historical importance of the City of the Dead. Members of these groups each have their own arguments for why the City of the Dead should be saved from demolition. These arguments demonstrate the complexity of the issues involved and are evidence of the significant numbers of people who will be affected by the decision of the government to proceed with its removal plans.

It now should be clear that the residents of the City of the Dead represent a spectrum of life experiences. Some of these people will welcome the government's proposals and plans wholeheartedly. Many of these people are living in conditions of such extreme poverty, they would be willing to take any risks in order to move into a city of the living. Others would welcome the idea but are justifiably skeptical of the government's abilities to fulfill its promises, especially those to find housing for the residents of the cemeteries. These people want some form of guarantee that they will be re-housed before they give up the only shelter they have. In this sense, they welcome the plans of the government in theory but fear them in practice. Most people of the City of the Dead would probably fall into this category.

The final group of residents of the City are quite comfortable with their lives in the cemeteries, and have become resigned to their position as tomb-dwellers. In rare cases, such residents favor their current situation over any alternatives. Whether out of a strong bond of love for a deceased family member, the time and resources invested in a life in the City of the Dead, or simply a genuine contentment with their lives, these residents have come to think of the City of the Dead as their home. For some, it is the only home that they have ever known. They wish to remain there until they are truly among the dead.

The real issue for most of the cemeteries' residents and tomb owners is compensation. The government recognizes that these two groups pose potential opposition to its plans and is therefore making promises of compensation. "Protestors will be one of two: either those who live in the City of the Dead itself, or those who own a tomb in one of its many cemeteries. Both will be compensated and assisted as free housing units will be provided for those who live in the cemeteries,"[38] says Governor Akher. Such promises, however, are falling on doubtful ears. Cemetery resident Fardoos Ahmed (see p. 108) looks at the aged piece of paper claiming that she is entitled to government housing, housing that never existed. She questions the government's intentions and will. She doesn't believe that these promises from the government will ever be carried out. Other residents agree. If the removal of the City of the Dead from Cairo proper is to be realized, many questions must first be answered. After years of being discriminated against, ignored, and marginalized, residents ask:

How could "free housing units" exist?

Will there be enough for everyone?

How will the amount of compensation be determined?

Will we be harassed when we apply for such housing?

What will we need to do to prove that we qualify for government housing?

How long will the re-housing process take?

Where will the housing be located?

Will we have to move to a satellite city where there may be

little employment opportunity?

Will we have access to such services as education, health care

and public transportation in the new location?

How will our personal relocation costs be paid for?

How much will it be?

What are the guarantees?
Will we really be better off?

Ideally, any new communities that residents are moved to by the government should include all of the services that attracted the rural-to-urban migrants to the city in the first place. Jobs with competitive wages should be available in the new location, as should services such as transportation, communication, and sanitation. There should also be easy access to health and educational facilities.

The situation is even more complicated for those people who have established informal enterprises in the cemeteries. Shop and factory owners and workers are afraid to concede both their shelter and their source of economic livelihood to the government. Tombkeepers and undertakers also find their trades threatened by the government's proposals.

Residents of the City of the Dead and tomb owners will not willfully agree to the relocation unless the government is able to answer their many questions to their satisfaction. The people of the City of the Dead have learned many lessons in their lives as informals. Trust of the government is not one of them. Many have experienced homelessness. All have found the doors to legal housing barred. These people are willing to put up a considerable struggle to protect the shelter they have worked hard to create for themselves.

Beyond the residents' many questions are those of the government's priorities:

Which is more important—reclaiming land in economically valuable locations or improving conditions for Cairo's urban poor?

Is the proposed re-housing of the City of the Dead's residents merely rhetoric created to justify the demolition plan and win its approval?

Are the potential human benefits first on the priority list, or do they rank behind the economic factors?

Is the plan rooted in a deep compassion for the society's indigent, or is it rooted in the desire for profit?

It will be a challenge for a government that often appears, in the eyes of many of the City of the Dead's residents, to be driven by a hunger for money and power. Few believe that the government could embark on such an ambitious project for purely humanitarian reasons.

The concerns of tomb owners will also have to be addressed. The owners not only expect to be compensated, but they protest being obliged to travel far out into the desert in order to visit tombs during feasts, holidays, and on weekends as well as for funerals.

Finally but importantly, scholars of Islam, Islamic art and architecture, and Middle Eastern history also oppose or have questions about the government's proposal. In essence, these professionals want to know if the important Islamic monuments of the cemeteries will benefit or suffer from the government's actions. They ask:

> Will the important Islamic mausolea and monuments of the City of the Dead be removed along with the family plots?
>
> If some are allowed to stay in their current places, who will decide which ones remain?
>
> What efforts will be made to preserve these monuments?
>
> Will these monuments be restored as part of the project?
>
> Will these monuments be developed as part of new tourism projects?
>
> Will these monuments be surrounded by new, modern apartment buildings and businesses?

Yet another question that will have to be addressed: Is it ethical to move the dead?

Equally important to the monuments' physical presence are the stories each one has hidden inside its walls. The monuments of the City of the Dead represent people, ideas, events, and centuries of achievements. Together, they tell the long history of Cairo, the Islamic city. They are memorials to past generations, reminders of distant times, and they form a bridge with the present. From this perspective, the government's plan will rob Cairo of an enormous archive. With the demolition of the City of the Dead will come the destruction of part of the capital city's past. Whereas the government wishes to remove the cemeteries from the heart of Cairo, historically this is their proper place. Will the next step be to move the pyramids to clear the way for urban expansion? Governor Akher claims that the City of the Dead is an "insult for every Egyptian."* On the contrary, Egyptians should look on the cemeteries with pride for the history they represent. The governor's assertion fails to recognize the area's historical and religious importance.

Any proposal of change for the City of the Dead must include measures to preserve the historical importance of the necropolises as well as efforts to serve the various needs of the cemeteries' population. In addition to

---

*Governor Akher's comments were made to journalist Ahmed Samy and appeared in *Transit Egypt*, issue 2, page 5.

solutions to the immediate problems, proposals should address the source of these problems. Urban planners need to question the very existence of life in the City of the Dead.

> Why are these people there?
> Why have they been unable to leave?
> What is fundamentally wrong with a system that has allowed this phenomenon to occur?

Only by solving these problems can the creation of future Cities of the Dead be avoided.

Although the situation of many of the people of the City of the Dead is desperate, a plan of help should not be hastily enacted. The merits and features of such a project need to be discussed and debated publicly and at length, so that the best solution can be achieved for all people involved. Details of the project must be clearly laid out so that all questions are answered. Otherwise, the government is likely to encounter strong opposition from the residents of the City of the Dead. Staunch opposition is also likely from Islamic scholars. In addition, the removal of Islamic mausolea to make room for business and tourism enterprises could strengthen the Islamic anti-government campaign.

The future of the City of the Dead remains uncertain. There may be no perfect solution to the developmental challenge it represents. It is only just, however, that any solution put the welfare of the living human beings who inhabit the cemeteries as its top priority. To do this, the government must look beyond the City of the Dead and its people to the root causes of the existence of this unique community. Moreover, any government plan must preserve and display the historical, aesthetic, architectural, and religious importance of the City of the Dead's mausolea and monuments.

STORIES

> I went to the courthouse and I asked the judge where he would propose that I go. Where should my eight homeless children go? I looked him directly in the eyes. I asked him "Will you give me an apartment?"
>
> —Fardoos Ahmed
> Resident of the Bab al-Nasr Cemetery

Poverty. More than anything else, poverty defines the existence of much of the community of the City of the Dead, and that is the first word that comes to mind when thinking about the Bab al-Nasr Cemetery. Somewhat isolated from the rest of the City of the Dead, the indigence of this area is also more pronounced than in the other cemeteries. Here it seems that almost all of the tombs are occupied by the living. Many people live in poorly constructed shanties made out of scraps of metal and wood built over or between tombs. This destitution is reflected in the disposition of many of the residents of this cemetery. More so than any other area, the people of Bab al-Nasr demonstrated a strong sense of fatalism, a complete lack of faith or hope in the future. They felt abandoned by their families, their government, their people, and they are drowning in their despair.

SALAH MOHAMED
The Cleopatra Salesman

Salah Mohamed can be found sitting on the ground in front of his tomb on the main street running through the Bab al-Nasr Cemetery. His brown galabeya is old, torn, soiled, and stinks of human excretion. In his lap are two new packs of Cleopatra brand cigarettes, which he hopes to sell to anyone who happens to be passing by. By his side is an old bamboo cane that he needs to walk after a leg injury left him partially crippled.

I feel like I've been sitting here all of my life. I've been here for so long that I've forgotten what life is like outside of the cemetery. Indeed, I've forgotten what my life was like before I came here. Of course, this is not life here. This is simply waiting to die. It's death on earth. I might as well be dead. What good am I doing here? Would anyone care if I were dead? I wouldn't. I would welcome it. What kind of life do I have? I haven't one. My life stopped eighteen years ago when I came to this horrible place, living with the dead. The dead of this world together with the dead of the next.

I didn't always live here. There was a time when I lived like a real person with a family and all. That seems like a whole other lifetime. I guess that it was. I lived in Bab al-Sharia, which actually isn't so far from here. I lived with my wife (God bless her) in the same rooms that my father and mother had lived in before us. It wasn't exactly a place for a prince or a pasha, but it was my home.

I had done a lot of odd jobs over the years in order to make ends meet. I always brought home enough to buy food for the family. We weren't rich, but we weren't hungry either. The last job that I worked at was doing body work on cars before they were re-painted. It was a good job. I enjoyed doing it, and it paid better than most of the work I had done.

Amina, my wife, was a good woman. God bless her. She was a good housekeeper and wife and was always there to fulfill my needs. We had lived together for more than thirty years, and we were still so happy with each other. I had no idea how quickly everything that I had achieved in my life would be destroyed.

Everything came crashing down eighteen years ago, seriously. I told you that the place where we were living was not exactly fit for a prince or a pasha. We didn't think it was so bad though. It was good enough for us to call home. I didn't know that it would be the last home I would ever have. Well, it was much worse than we thought. It turns out it wasn't fit for anybody. The walls had been laden with cracks and, at one point, government inspectors condemned the building and told us to move out. We never really believed that it was that bad, however, and ignored the warnings. There were a lot of other buildings in the area that were the same way. Some even seemed to be worse. So, we continued living there patching things up where and when we could.

It was early one morning in the winter of 1975 when I awoke to a strange rumbling sound. All of a sudden, everything started to shake violently. I knew immediately what was happening. The building was falling down! I have never been so scared in my life. It was such a strange feeling. It wasn't as if I was really taking part in it. It was as if I were somewhere up in the air looking down at what was happening. I saw myself scream to Amina to get up and to get out of the house. I saw myself scrambling for safety. Then, I saw the ceiling crashing down on top of us.

My wife was killed in the collapse (God bless her soul). I escaped with my leg injured badly. People told me I was lucky; God had saved me. I don't feel that way at all. I feel as if I am being punished. I can never forgive myself for what happened to Amina, and I feel I am being punished for it by being allowed to live.

After the incident I was barely able to walk, and I was unable to work. Of course I felt that I had nothing left to work for anyway. Amina was gone. I didn't have anything left to live for. The government gave me a certificate and told me I would be housed in a subsidized apartment after two months. I moved here (to the cemetery) while I was waiting for that to happen. As I said, that was eighteen years ago. I gave up waiting a long time ago!

So, here I am a seventy-year-old man just sitting here on the roadside watching the people going by and hoping that someone will buy my cigarettes. Sometimes I also sell green boughs from trees to people who are coming to visit the dead. They leave them at the tombs as an offering. I live alone in my one room, and I don't really bother with anybody unless they bother with me. I mostly just sit. I don't eat very well because food is expensive and I haven't got money. Also, I haven't got anyone to cook and to clean for me. Sometimes my neighbors will give me extra bits of food and tea. They're kind people. They gave me my food today. We'll have to wait and see where it will come from tomorrow. Would you like to buy some cigarettes?

MOHAMED MOUSA
Hatred of Life and of the Living

Mohamed Mousa's story is short. He is a man of very few words. "I hate everything in this life" are among the first words he will speak upon meeting someone. He can be seen straying among the tombs of the Bab al-Nasr Cemetery with an old, broken broom in each hand. He sweeps off the tombstones as he passes, pushing dust up into the air. He hopes to be rewarded with a few piasters for this unnecessary service he provides warily and which has become his life.

It's better than begging. At least I am trying to do something for the money people give to me. I also collect garbage in the cemetery, and I sell it to people who can recycle it or use it. I also help the undertaker from this area in conducting burials. I can get more money from that than from anything else.

I live here by myself. I am not married and I never have been. I don't like women. In fact, I don't like people. Most people are bad. They will pretend to be your friends and then they will stab you in the back, even if they are your own flesh and blood. It is better to live with the dead people. They don't talk to you. They can't give you anything bad.

I haven't always lived in the cemetery. I wasn't always this bitter about life or about people until I learned better. I was born here in Cairo, but my family comes from a village near Tanta [a city in the Nile Delta region]. We had an apartment in Daher nearby. It was my family's apartment, but my mother and father died when they were still young and I became part owner along with my older brother. I lived there with him and his family. My brother and I never got along very well but we co-existed. After all, we were brothers (or so I thought). That term doesn't mean much to me anymore because I have no more family.

My brother had always been smarter than me. He had learned to read and write, whereas I only learned to write my name. I don't know if I can even remember to do that now. Anyway, in those days, I really didn't think that it mattered how much education you had. My brother made it matter though. I knew that he wasn't happy with my living with him and his family, but I didn't have the money at the time to go any place else. Still, his wife used to complain a lot about having to share the space. I would have liked to move but I couldn't, and there was no way to split the apartment into two. My brother asked me to leave on more than one occasion but I stayed. The apartment belonged to both of us, and I had as much of a right to be there as he. Even though he was uncomfortable with this situation (we both were) I never expected him to do what he did!

One day he showed me a paper and said it was very important and that it was about the inheritance of the apartment from our parents upon their death. He said I had to sign it along with him in order to show the government who owned the apartment, as the deed had never been changed after my father's death. He showed me where he had signed the paper and where I should sign. Unable to read, I signed on the blind trust of my brother and didn't think about it again. It was only afterwards I found out the true contents of the document I had signed, and learned that my brother had made a fool of me. I had signed a paper giving him full ownership of the apartment! Can you imagine that! Someone with the same blood, the same genes, as me!

I was shocked. It still makes me so angry to this day to think about what he did to me. I guess if you look at how horrible the world is nowadays my story is not so surprising. At the time, however, I was naive. There was nothing I could do. I left without much of a fight. At that point I just wanted to get away. I never wanted to see him or hear his name again. I didn't want to try and stay. Not after what he had done. Still, I didn't have any place to go. I couldn't afford to live any place, except here (in the cemetery). This is where I came and where I have been ever since. I'm living with the dead and waiting for the day when I am one of them, free of this horrible world.

I live alone and mostly wander around from place to place in the cemetery. I don't bother with anyone except the undertaker who comes to find me when he needs help. I wish more people would die so that he would call me more often and I would have more money to buy things (although I don't need very much).

I eat what I find or I buy some vegetables. I don't eat very well but it doesn't bother me so much. I guess I've grown used to that empty feeling. Perhaps I will die quicker. Of course some of the families who live here will *give me food when they can. Visitors will also give me food or a little money. I don't know why they do. I wouldn't give anything to anyone for free in this world. Nothing is for free in this life, only the air we breathe, and in Cairo that doesn't mean too much. It's miserable, absolutely miserable.*

FARDOOS AHMED
Hell on Earth

Fardoos Ahmed sits outside in an old gutted-out wardrobe and passes her time with the other women who live in her area of the Bab al-Nasr Cemetery. They have nothing good to say. They can't remember the last time that they felt true happiness. They have no hope.

I remember playing in the fields as a young child in the village of Abu Shuay in the Fayyum district of Middle Egypt. I think those memories probably represent the brief time in my life when I felt happiness. I was young, free, and without responsibilities. I got married when I was fifteen and that brought major changes in my life and the beginning of my hardship and despair. My new husband decided not to try to make it as a farmer as all of his and my ancestors had done before us. He decided that we would move to the city. I think he came to regret this decision to leave the countryside. I know that I certainly did. Of course I never had much say in the matter. I was just allowed to stand beside him, agree, and be supportive. I learned quickly that my husband was a risk-taker, and he joined all of the other young men who were going to the city in search of opportunity. He took me with him to start a new life in this strange and horrible environment.

I remember being so afraid as the bus approached Cairo and began to weave through its crowded streets. I had never left the shelter of my village before and didn't know that such a world existed as that which Cairo held. Sure, I was with my new husband but he was almost as much of a stranger to me as this new, strange place! Tall buildings, cars, people, noise, pollution . . . all of the things I take for granted now overwhelmed me when I came here as a bint al balad [country girl]. I had only a few belongings with me, which I had been given as wedding presents. My husband had even fewer coins with him. This is what we were to start our new life with. We were crazy!

While we adjusted to our new environment (Have I ever really adjusted?), we slept on the floor of an apartment belonging to a couple from our area who had made the journey to the city a couple of years earlier. Already I felt alone. I remember trembling the first night that I slept in Cairo. I didn't

The Future

sleep at all. I spent the first night trying to hold back tears so that I wouldn't embarrass my husband in front of our hosts.

Mohamed, my husband, was determined to make a better life for us, especially when he found out that I was pregnant. We should have waited to have children, but you know how these things happen. Anyway, it wasn't my choice. In fact, I never should have brought any children into this horrible world. Instead, I had eight! I gave birth to four sons and four daughters. People used to tell me that I was blessed to have so many children, but what kind of a life was I providing for them?

Our stay on the floor of our friends' apartment lasted for a few months until Mohamed was able to save up enough money for us by working odd jobs to rent an apartment. The rent was LE 6 pounds every month for a two room flat in a poor but decent area of the city. What I would give to live there now!

I was now in charge of a household, and I was grateful for the help and education that I had received on life in the city while we were staying with friends. I would watch my husband go from job to job, the years pass by, and my eight children being brought into the world from my womb. Throughout all of this, I would try to stretch out the food and money so that there would be enough for everyone to eat, even if I had to go hungry myself. Sometimes the children and I would all have to fast for a day or two in order to conserve. Occasionally I would borrow from friends but my husband would be furious with me if he found out and curse me for the shame I brought on the family. Early on I had to sell the gold bracelets and the ring he had given to me as a wedding present. He promised to buy me new ones when times got better, but those times never came. I did have hope though that things would improve. That is until my husband became ill and died suddenly. That was twenty years ago.

Mohamed's death was devastating for me and for all of the family. I was so scared. I was a widow with eight children! I was lonelier and more afraid than I had ever been in my life. My eldest son went to work to provide for the family, but that wasn't enough. Soon we found that we couldn't afford to eat and to pay the rent for the apartment. After all, we had just barely been making ends meet when Mohamed was alive. We were forced out onto the streets. I remember the cold nights we spent there as if they were just days ago. We would sleep in doorways and on street corners at night and be humiliated by begging for food and change during the day. Our only option was the cemetery. At that time it was becoming a place where a lot of desperate people like us were settling.

At first, I refused to live with the dead. I had never heard of a more disgusting suggestion. Only the hope that it would be a temporary situation gave me the courage to move there among the tombs. Look where I am twenty years later! I am still here, but all of my hope has died along with my spirit and will.

The structure into which Fardoos and her family moved was an old wooden room built over a tomb in the Bab al-Nasr area of the City of the Dead. Over the years, the structure has been patched with scraps of different materials and looks like a shanty. There is no running water, no bathroom, no decoration. A wire run in from the street allows a single light bulb to light the room dimly at night. Over the years, another make-shift room has appeared beside the original. Along with Fardoos and her family, geese and chickens are scattered throughout the two rooms and on the dusty earth outside.

When I moved here I agreed to pay the tomb's owner sixty piasters every month. The owner, however, later changed her mind and attempted to have us removed from the tomb. I was determined not to be put back out on the streets again! I fought the law. I refused to leave, and she took legal action against me. The police tried to force us to move but I refused. I have been summoned to appear in court three times. Each time I have succeeded in keeping shelter for my family. I couldn't afford a lawyer to represent us, of course, but I have my mind and my big mouth and that is all the defense I need. I'm better than any lawyer. A lawyer could never understand what I feel. I went to the courthouse and I asked the judge where he would propose that I go. Where should my eight homeless children go? I looked him directly in the eyes. I asked him "Will you give me an apartment?"

Fardoos has been able to keep shelter over her children's (now all fully grown) heads and food in their mouths in spite of the dire conditions in which they live. She even worked out of her tomb-home for a period of time while her youngest boys were growing up. She remembers these days as the darkest of her life. In traditional Egypt, waged work by women is a last resort and an enormous source of disrespect for her and her family. She has had to and continues to sacrifice.

If I have one egg and my daughters and sons have none, I will give it to them and go hungry for them. I do sacrifice. Still, I feel as if I have failed as a mother. After I die I know that my children will say horrible things about me. They will ask "Why did she have us? Why did she bring us into this world without money? Without anything?" I have been unable to provide for my children. Of course I am going to hell.

School was a luxury Fardoos' children were unable to enjoy. Only the two oldest girls received any significant education, with one finishing primary school and another advancing to preparatory. The boys were forced to contribute to the family economy at an early age. All of the children dream of getting jobs in the Arab countries of the Persian Gulf, joining thousands of other Egyptian migrant laborers. None of Fardoos' children, however, have succeeded in escaping the cemetery.

My oldest daughter is beautiful and attracted a young man from outside of the cemetery. The man had made his intention of marriage clear to her and to us and we had begun to dream of the life ahead for my fortunate daughter. God had looked upon her kindly. Our dreams were short-lived, however. When the mother of the groom-to-be found out that the girl her son wished to marry was from the cemetery (a fact he had kept hidden from her), she was horrified and refused to agree to such an arrangement. Without the blessing of his mother, the marriage was called off and our dreams were shattered as well as the heart of my beautiful daughter.

My youngest daughter met with a similar fate even though she became engaged to a man from the cemetery. The couple became engaged four years ago, but they still have not married. They love each other so much but simply do not have the money to go any further. They keep waiting for the day when he will find decent work. The young man has repeatedly tried to get a visa and job in a Gulf country, but he hasn't had any success. Today, the poor can't afford even to get married!

Fatima, another of Fardoos' daughters, also wants a job in a Persian Gulf country. Unlike her sisters, Fatima succeeded in finding marriage, but it has not led to the life she expected. Fatima lives with her husband in the Bab al-Nasr Cemetery quite near to her mother and the tomb where she spent her later childhood years. Her husband works as an assistant to an undertaker. He leaves in the morning, is gone all of the day, and doesn't always come home at night. Any money he may have made is typically long gone before he arrives home.

Fatima begins:

I hope that he never comes home again. He is no good. He says that he is too ashamed to bring his friends here so that they see where he lives and what would they do anyway, sit on the dirt floor and drink tea? I ask him who's fault it is that we live in such conditions. It sure isn't mine. So, he spends all of his times in coffee houses and I don't know where else. He wastes all of his money on cigarettes, drinks, and his friends. He probably even gambles too. He never stops to think about his wife and children who go hungry.

She continues:

I only want an apartment. If someone wants to have sex with me for money I will go to him. I have already lost my pride living here in this hell-hole and in this way. I want to be a prostitute for rich Arabs from the Persian Gulf. I could get an apartment with the money I would make. I could leave this place and change my life. I would be willing to do it for the opportunity for change.

Fardoos echoes her daughter's words:

I only want an apartment so that I can live with a sense of decency. We don't even have a bathroom. We have to squat down and go between the tombs. Can you imagine this? What if someone sees me accidentally? It is humiliating! I cry all of the time, but what can I do? What difference does it make?

The only way to escape the death of the cemetery is to die. In the cemetery, death is always around. One particular incident stands out in Fardoos' mind:

A number of years ago the son of the owner of the tomb was killed suddenly in a car accident. Without any warning, a funeral showed up at the tomb to bury the boy beneath my very feet! I was so frightened! I really couldn't imagine sleeping with the body of that young boy underneath me. I was especially afraid because he did not die a natural death. When someone dies unnaturally, they may have an evil spirit which is free to roam. I was afraid for my children. When no one was looking, I put a knife in the tomb with him. It was the only knife I had, but I was willing to go without it to protect my family from the devil. The devil is afraid of fire, horseshoes, and knives.

Fardoos has no hope for the future. She has a paper from the government dated 1973, which claims that her family would be given subsidized housing.

Sadat talked about a new city for all of us with government apartments and utilities. Of course nothing ever happened. I have also heard rumors that Mubarak plans to move and re-house all of the people of the cemetery.

The Future

Two years ago I was interviewed by a group of people from a French company who claimed that they were going to move the people of the cemetery and build hotels and gardens in the area. They took my name and picture with them but nothing has happened. I have been left behind. Twenty years of hopes and promises have passed me by. I have no more faith. It is enough.

I was especially angry after the earthquake happened.* The victims of the earthquake all have new apartments. It was so easy for the government to give them housing. What about us? We live with dead people! Some of the earthquake victims even had money in the bank or other apartments. We have nothing. The government took care of them while I sit here in the cemetery leading a disgusting life. I am already in hell!

*An earthquake measuring 5.9 on the Richter scale rocked Cairo in October 1992.

CONCLUSION

> The City of the Dead has become an emblem of one of Cairo's less glorious accomplishments. In a city where millions live in slums or one-room apartments, in shanties built on rooftops or in the rooms once reserved for the guardians of tombs, upward of a million apartments stand empty.
>
> —Ed Kashi

I have tried not to romanticize the City of the Dead. These vast and ancient necropolises that have grown up near the center of Cairo have become possibly the largest cemetery group in the world. It has become not only an eternal home for the dead, but also an archive of Cairo's history and a home to hundreds of thousands of Cairo's urban poor. The communities formed by these masses of people, once thought to be temporary, have become permanent residential neighborhoods marked on Cairene maps. These people have responded in a creative way to provide their own housing after finding the doors to legal, formal shelter closed to them. Such doors have to be opened if the fundamental problems symbolized by the modern face of the City of the Dead are to be truly resolved.

The Muslim cemeteries of the City of the Dead are virtually as old as Islam in Egypt. The cemeteries provided the original burial grounds for the Arab invaders of the Seventh century. Over more than a thousand years, the cemeteries have continued to be used and expanded by each succeeding band of rulers. This Muslim burial ground is unique in the Islamic world as Islam adapted to pre-existing burial practices. One major aspect of this adaptation is the use of the cemetery as a functioning part of the community. The City of the Dead was never only for the dead. There has always been life among the dead in Cairo. The cemeteries have traditionally been home to guardians of tombs and reciters of qu'ran. The poor, the sick, and criminals have always sought refuge there. Sufi monks chose to build their monasteries in the heart of the cemeteries, and Mamluke leaders built their mosques and funerary complexes around the tombs complete with shops, mills, rooms for travelers to rent, and schools.

Today, Cairo suffers from a severe and chronic lack of adequate and affordable housing. Cairo's urban poor, a group that includes established city dwellers as well as migrants from Egypt's countryside, have often found that the avenues toward obtaining legal, formal housing are not accessible to them. Increasingly, legal housing is a privilege enjoyed only by those with a certain degree of economic and political power. The poor have found themselves forced to compete for basic necessities, not only against other people, but against the system itself. Many have found that they are better off outside of the law.

The City of the Dead is an informal community. The majority of the housing currently being created in Egypt is informal. This housing has been instrumental in maintaining parity between Egypt's swelling population and units of available housing. Informal housing is housing that is built or exists in contravention to building codes and zoning laws. This makes the City of the Dead an illegal society. Informal housing is also less well equipped than formal, legal housing and composes most of the slum housing in Cairo.

Most of the inhabitants of the City of the Dead are first, second, or third generation rural-to-urban migrants. As the gap between the city and the countryside has grown, and as the land has increasingly failed to support the growing population, they have come to the city in search of increased access to education, health care, transportation, communication, and better wages. This is a common phenomenon faced by developing countries throughout the world. Such migration has contributed to Cairo's overurbanization—its inability to meet the growing population's needs by expanding and bettering socio-economic conditions.

A result of these migration patterns has been the ruralization of the city. As these rural migrants flock to the city, they tend to preserve the socio-cultural patterns of their towns and villages of origin. Areas of informal housing such as the City of the Dead are communities in which the lifestyle and

Conclusion

traditions of the majority of the residents are in many ways identical to those of rural Egypt.

Residents who live in the informal sector tend to work in the informal sector as well. That is, economic activities are not officially noticed through registration and taxation procedures. The residents of the cemeteries can be seen selling tissues or newspapers on the streets or operating and working in unlicensed shops or factories in the cemeteries. While providing a source of income, the informal economy offers unreliable employment and low social mobility, as well as the constant threat of apprehension by authorities for engaging in activities that are officially illegal, a concern repeatedly voiced by cemetery residents whose complete existence is in the informal sector.

The cemeteries have long been thought of as a place where convicts and run-aways seek refuge from authority. Given few choices and little opportunity, some of the City of the Dead's residents resort to crime, in particular the sale of drugs, to alleviate their poverty. The cemeteries are also seen as potential breeding grounds for Islamic fundamentalism.

The government of Egypt is attempting to address the City of the Dead and the problems that it represents. A plan has been exhorted by the government that will move the cemeteries out of Cairo and onto the desert Cairo-Suez road and re-house the cemeteries' residents in subsidized apartments. The residents of the City of the Dead, however, view the government's plans with skepticism and fear. These people seek guarantees that they will be adequately compensated if such proposals are implemented.

The government's plan fails to connect the problems represented by the cemetery communities to the deeper problems facing Egypt: the economy's inability to create jobs and affordable housing for a large portion of its population. Informal sectors exist where governments avoid necessary structural changes in their economies. In Egypt, the government has (to date) largely chosen to ignore or police informal activity. However, attempts to control the informal sector largely fail because the key to such control lies in making the very existence of an informal sector unnecessary.

Numerous theories of how to combat the systematic problems of the Egyptian economy and thus improve the well-being of millions of Egyptians living below the poverty line have been advanced and their merits and shortfalls have been discussed and debated in public forums. Development theorists have drawn upon the successes and failures of the many other underdeveloped nations, which also face the massive problems that Egypt is presently confronting. They have also drawn upon the lessons learned

Laundry is hung to dry over grave stones in the Cemetery of the Great.

from a growing number of studies on informality conducted throughout the developing world.

There appears to be a growing consensus that, in the short-term, governments must upgrade areas of informal housing such as the City of the Dead in order to provide temporary relief to the inhabitants until thoughtful solutions can be implemented. In Egypt, the government has already been forced to upgrade its services to some areas of the City of the Dead, and it has installed such infrastructure as electricity, telephones, and running water to parts of the cemeteries.

In the long-term, the Egyptian government must make the process of acquiring affordable formal housing easier by simplifying the system and making it more accessible to people with little education (the bureaucratic system in Egypt is a challenge for even the most educated Egyptians). Whereas the costs and detriments associated with informality are great, government regulations often make the cost of becoming formal even greater.

The challenges facing Egypt are enormous: The number of affordable, formal sector housing units must be increased. The economy must be able

Conclusion

to produce real employment for millions of underemployed and unemployed Egyptians To control rural-to-urban migration, improvements must be made in the transportation, communication, health care, employment, compensation, and educational standards of towns and villages throughout Egypt. The crisis in agriculture must be addressed. The gap between rural and urban standards of living must be decreased so that rural and semi-rural Egypt will become more attractive places to live and work.

As long as it is perceived that urban areas provide more opportunities and a more comfortable life, migration to Cairo from the Egyptian countryside will continue, a migration that the city will remain unable to support. These migrants are in search of higher wages, stable work, increased educational opportunities, as well as better health care, sanitation and recreational facilities.

Egypt has a highly polarized investment system, which reflects the government's urban bias. This policy must be changed, and rural economies need to be stimulated to provide job opportunities, better services, and to allow physical infrastructure to be improved. Secondary cities must also be developed, to help slow the one-step migration of rural-to-urban migrants. Currently, Cairo has three million more inhabitants than Egypt's fourteen secondary cities combined.

The above outline of the challenges faced by Egypt is a gross oversimplification. The magnitude of the challenges ahead for the country is enormous. The objective of this book, however, is not to offer solutions to the fundamental problems plaguing Egypt's economy. Such a daunting task warrants the space of every page written here. It will suffice to say that to truly change the system and provide a decent quality of life for every Egyptian will require a multitude of patience, sacrifice, hard work, and money.

There has been much discussion among development theorists, government officials, and scholars regarding the concrete steps that need to be taken to improve the Egyptian economy. Yet, the dilemma of the people of the City of the Dead cannot be solved simply by improving Egypt's economy. Rather, there is another area that needs to be addressed when looking toward the future of the residents of the City of the Dead; an area that is more abstract than tangible economic reforms. Indeed, few people have seriously considered the changes in attitude by the Egyptian government and people that must take place for real, sustainable development to occur. Such abstract changes are just as vital as, and must coincide with, the concrete structural adjustments that the government will take. In short, not only do the economic and political systems of Egypt have to change, but the Egyptian people themselves have to change as well. The concrete and the abstract must go hand-in-hand, each facilitating the other's ultimate success. Solutions to the daunting tasks outlined in the summary above, solutions that will benefit the lives of the residents of Cairo's City of the Dead, cannot simply be handed down to the people by the government of Egypt. Rather, Egyptians must subscribe to and endow any national goals that strive to better their lives. Egyptians need to feel a sense of empowerment and believe that their actions and initiative can have a direct effect on the conditions of Egyptian society. Those who have become disillusioned with the society in which they live need a sense of hope.

Such changes in attitude and outlook, however, will be difficult to achieve in a society such as Egypt that has profoundly authoritarian roots. Such a transformation will only come with real democratic change and the creation of a true civil society.

An integral part of this change in attitude and empowerment of the people must be the acceptance of a greater degree of equality among Egyptians and a greater sense of responsibility and respect for one another's well-being. As stated earlier, Egyptian society has a rigid social class system, and there is very little social mobility. Among Egyptians, there is widespread belief that, in society, there are people who are naturally in the upper, middle, and lower classes, and there are those who are condemned to lives of impoverishment. The latter are frequently blamed for their own grim circumstances. Indeed, the residents of the City of the Dead are often blamed for their own poverty by people claiming that the cause of their destitution is their lack of skills and ambition. Yet, one has only to look at their informal activities to refute such charges. The imaginative response that these people have shown in the face of homelessness and indigence demonstrates that they have initiative. What they are lacking is not ambition. Rather, it is opportunity. While outsiders will ask "How can they live there?" The real questions that need to be addressed are "Have they been given any real alternative?" "Have they had any choice?"

Egyptain government and society must not view the City of the Dead simply as a problem area as they have in the past. The people of the cemeteries have created their own existence in an illegal society. They have created their own shelter and have survived, often in the face of enormous odds. What has happened in the City of the Dead is a positive response by migrants and poor urban dwellers to a deficiency in affordable housing and a deficiency in real employment in the modern, capital-intensive sector. Instead of an isolated problem area, the City of the Dead is actually a symptom of a wider systematic breakdown. When viewed as such, it is clear

Conclusion

that its victims need support from the government and from society rather than continued harassment and neglect.

The government and people of Egypt need to bring the inhabitants of the City of the Dead into the twentieth century. They need to make them feel that they have not been forgotten. The tomb-dwellers of the City of the Dead need to perceive that they are not being blamed for their own meager existence.

The plight of the hundreds of thousands of Egyptians who have made their homes in the City of the Dead must be recognized and acknowledged by society. Once the people of the City of the Dead are given this dignity, then they can be treated as fellow citizens and given the rights accorded to them. Acceptance of the City of the Dead and its people would rid the residents of some of the stigma attached to them and pave the way for the return of their hope in the future. Instead of condemning a large portion of the population to lives of destitution and indigence, Egyptian society needs to reach out to these people and believe that they have the same rights as those more fortunate.

When addressing the development challenge presented by the City of the Dead, any concrete step that is taken to combat the enormous problems symbolized by this unique informal community must be accompanied by a corresponding change in the psychological outlook of the people. To establish this, Egyptians must first be introduced to a culture of democratic values. It is not enough to merely read about it on paper. Egyptians must feel that they have the right to make choices; the right to control their own destinies. Only then can sustainable development take place. Of course, the government can impose reforms from above. Without the support of the people however, such reforms are ultimately doomed to failure.

The City of the Dead is a unique community in Cairo and the world. It is home to more than 1,200 years of Islamic history, some of the most beautiful and intriguing monuments in the Muslim world, and it is a curious informal community of rural-to-urban migrants, established urban poor, and their offspring. At the same time, however, it is but a small part of a larger problem that haunts Egypt and many other developing countries. The quandary of people living among tombs and the problems that are symbolized by their meager existence cannot be solved by moving the cemeteries into the desert as the government suggests. They cannot simply be solved by resettling the residents into subsidized, formal housing units. Such actions amount to little more than policing activities. The problems lie much deeper, and the solutions are much greater. It is clear, however, that there is no perfect or simple answer to the challenges represented by the City of the

Dead and the multifaceted world within its borders. Indeed, there is no one solution that will please everybody. The first challenge confronting the Egyptian government and people is, however, to understand the complex nature of the City of the Dead and its relationship to the world outside of the cemeteries. I hope that by writing these pages, I have, in some small way, contributed to the accomplishment of that task.

Glossary of Arabic Terms

ablaq	striped, colored masonry
arabesque	ornamental design based on vegetal forms in which leaves and stems form a reciprocal, continuous interlacing pattern
baraka	blessing or good luck usually associated with a holy person or holy site
caliph	successor to the Prophet
duxla	the final stage in Egyptian courtship
falaheen	peasant farmers
fatha	the second stage of Egyptian courtship
hanouti	a person who oversees a large area of a cemetery
haram	something forbidden by Islam
howsh	a courtyard
iltifaq	the first stage of Egyptian courtship
kat b'kkitab	the fourth stage of Egyptian courtship
khanqah	residential institution especially endowed for Sufis
kufic	the earliest style of Arabic script
kuttab	Quaranic school

liwan	vaulted spaces surrounding the courtyard of a madrasa
madrasa	theological school
mashrabiyya	wooden lattice windows or screens with lace grill work
mihrab	the niche that indicates the direction of Mecca and prayer
minaret	the tower from which the call to prayer is made
minbar	pulpit from which the address at the Friday noon prayer is given
mulid	religious fair in celebration of a saint's birthday
rab'	apartment building or tenement
Ramadan	the Muslim holy month that commemorates the revelation of the Qu'ran to the Prophet Muhammad
sabil	public drinking fountain
shabka	the third stage of Egyptian courtship
sheesha	waterpipe
Sufi	Muslim ascetics bound to lead a communal life of prayer and poverty
zabaleen	garbage collectors
zawiya	a residence for Muslim Sufis centered around a sheikh
ziyyarah	visitation of a holy shrine

NOTES

INTRODUCTION

1. S. Lane-Poole. *A History of Egypt in the Middle Ages*, 2nd ed. New York: Methuen Press, 1914.

CHAPTER 1: THE PHYSICAL AND SOCIAL GROWTH OF THE CEMETERIES

2. Gaston Weit. *Cairo: City of Art and Commerce*, Norman: University of Oklahoma Press, 1964, p. 13. Translation by Seymour Feiler.

3. Janet Abu-Lughod. *Cairo: 1001 Years of the City Victorious*, New Jersey: Princeton University Press, 1971, p. 63.

4. Yasser Amr. "Life in Fatimid Cairo," *Places in Egypt,* Jan/Feb 1994, p. 45.

5. Gaston Weit, p. 67–68.

6. *Ibid.*, p. 69.

7. Dorothea Russell. *Medieval Cairo and the Monasteries of Wadi Natrun: A Historical Guide*, London: Weidenfield and Nicolson, 1962, p. 220.

8. Abu-Lughod, p. 129.

9. *Ibid.*, p. 129.

10. *Ibid.*, p. 195–96.

CHAPTER 2: THE MODERN ERA: INFORMAL HOUSING IN THE CITY OF THE DEAD

11. Abt Associates, Dames & Moore Inc., and the General Organization for Housing, Building & Planning Research (Egypt). "Informal Housing in Egypt," January 1982, p. xvi.

12. *Ibid.*, p. xvi.

13. Hernando De Soto. *The Other Path*, New York: Harper & Row, 1989, p. 24.

14. Abt Associates, p. xviii.

15. Mamoun Fandy. "The Tensions Behind the Violence in Egypt," *Middle East Policy*, No. 1, 1993, p. 29.

16. Jehan Sadat. *A Woman of Egypt*, New York: Simon & Schuster, 1987, p. 316.

17. Saad Eddin Ibrahim. "Urbanization in the Arab World," *Arab Society*, Cairo: AUC Press, 1985, p. 137.

18. Jehan Sadat, p. 316.

19. Hernando De Soto, p. xiii.

20. Ahmed El-Ghouri. "The Multiple Problems of Polygamy," *Al-Ahram Weekly*, 9–15 April 1992, p. 14.

21. Helen Watson. *Women in the City of the Dead*, Trenton, NJ: Africa World Press, 1992, p. 6

22. *Ibid.*, p. 5.

23. Hatem J. Rushdy. "The Disinherited," *Cairo Today*, Feb., 1992, p. 75.

24. Mostafa Kharoufi. "The Informal Dimension of Urban Activity in Egypt: Some Recent Work," *Cairo Papers on Social Science*, Cario: AUC Press, Vol. 14., Monograph 4, Winter 1991, p. 16.

25. Abu-Lughod, p. 196.

26. Abu-Lughod, p. 196.

27. Mostafa Kharoufi, p. 17.

28. Steve Negus. "Dead Show: Saints in Cemeteries," *The Middle East Times*, Vol. xi., No. 21, 25–31 May 1993, p. 8.

29. This comment was taken from an interview with Dr. Nadia el-Saftey in July 1992.

30. Jehan Sadat, p. 170.

31. This comment was taken from an interview with Dr. Nadia el-Saftey in July 1992.

32. Naguib Mahfouz. *The Thief and the Dogs*, Cairo: AUC Press, 1984, p. 61. Translation by Trevor Gassick & M. M. Badawi, Revised by John Rodenbeck.

CHAPTER 3: THE FUTURE OF THE CITY OF THE DEAD

33. Ahmed Samy. "Death of the City of the Dead," *Transit Egypt*, No. 2, Spring 1993, p. 5.

34. *Ibid.*, p. 5.
35. *Ibid.*, p. 5.
36. Abu-Lughod, p. 197.
37. Abu-Lughod, p. 197.
38. Ahmed Samy, p. 5.

SELECTED BIBLIOGRAPHY

Abdallah, Mohamed. "Slum Areas, Slum Education." *Al-Ahram Weekly* (23–29 July 1994): 6.
Abt Associates, Dames & Moore Inc., and the General Organization for Housing, Building and Planning Research (Egypt). "Informal Housing in Egypt," January 1992.
Abu-Lughod, Janet. *Cairo: 1001 Years of the City Victorious*, Princeton, NJ: Princeton University Press, 1971.
Amr, Yasser. "Life in Fatimid Cairo." *Places in Egypt* (Jan/Feb 1994): 40–45.
Anderson, Robert, and Ibrahim Fawzy (eds). *Egypt in 1800: Scenes from Napoleon's Description De L'Egypte*, London: English Library, 1987.
Apostolou, Andrew. "Vanishing Christians." *The Middle East* (January 1992): 24.
Chittock, Lorraine. "All Work and No Play." *Cairo Today* (December 1992): 106–10.
"Cutting Off the Supplies to Extremism." *The Egyptian Gazette* (December 8, 1992): 3.
De Soto, Hernando. *The Other Path*, New York: Harper & Row, 1989.
"Drifting Apart." *The Middle East* (June 1992): 23.
El-Bahr, Shar. "Restructuring Employment and Unemployment." *Al-Ahram Weekly* (7–13 May 1992): 5.
El-Ghouri, Ahmed. "The Multiple Problems of Polygamy." *Al-Ahram Weekly* (9–15 April 1992): 10.
Fandy, Mamoun. "The Tensions Behind the Violence in Egypt." *Middle East Policy* (1993): 25–30.

Fathi, Tarek. "Rotten Smell Rising from Bloody Rubble." *The Egyptian Gazette* (October 21, 1992): 7.
Fathi, Tarek. "Tying and Untying the Knot." *Al-Ahram Weekly* (February 27, 1992): 10.
Ginnochio, Robert. "A Walk Through the City of the Dead." *Places in Egypt* (July/August 1992): 43–46.
Handoussa, Heba and Gillian Potter (eds). *Employment and Structural Adjustment: Egypt in the 1990s,* Cairo: International Labour Organization, Suitz, AUC Press, 1991.
Hedges, Chris. "Egyptian Doctors Limit Kidney Transplants." *New York Times International* (January 23, 1992): A5.
Hopkins, Nicholas S. (ed). "Informal Sector in Egypt." *Cairo Papers in Social Science*, Vol. 14, Monograph 4, Cairo: AUC Press, Winter 1991.
Hubbell, Steve. "Fundamentalist Gains." *The Middle East International* (Sept. 25, 1992): 11.
Hubbell, Steve. "Tremors After the Earthquake." *The Middle East International* (October 23, 1992): 9.
Ibrahim, Saad Eddin. "Urbanization in the Arab World." *Arab Society: Social Science Perspectives,* Cairo: AUC Press, 1985 (123–47).
Karim, Shahinda. "City of the Dead." *Egypt's Travel and Recreation Guide* (1993 edition): 64–71, 167–73.
Keath, Lee. "New Order." *Egypt Today* (May 1994): 132–37, 145–46.
Khedi, Mohsen. "Suicidal Like the Whales." *Al-Ahram Weekly* (8–14 October 1992): 5.
Lane-Poole, S. *A History of Egypt in the Middle Ages,* 2nd ed. New York: Methuen Press, 1914.
Leunes, Alexia. "Heavy Breathing." *Cairo Today* (October 1992): 115–19, 135.
Leunes, Alexia. "The More the Merrier." *Cairo Today* (March 1992): 78–80, 113–15.
Mabrouk, Mirette. "Home Truths." *Cairo Today* (November 1992): 70–76, 114.
Moorehead, Alan. *The Blue Nile*, London: New English Library, 1982.
Nashat, Rajia. "Silent Killer Stalks the Nation." *Al-Ahram Weekly* (8–14 October 1992): 12.
Negus, Steve. "All Wrapped Up and Nowhere to Go." *The Middle East Times* (8–14 June 1993, November 23, 1993): 8.
Negus, Steve. "Dead Show: Saints in Cemeteries." *The Middle East Times* (25–31 May 1993): 8.
Negus, Steve. "Slum Upgrade Accelerates." *The Middle East Times* (10–16 January 1994): 1–2.
Negus, Steve. "Though I Walk Through the City of the Dead, I Shall Fear No Evil." *The Middle East Times* (1–7 June 1993): 8.
"Nightmare of the Teeming Millions." *The Middle East* (August 1992): 6.

Selected Bibliography

Oldham, Linda, Haguer El Hadid, and Hussein Tamaa. "Informal Communities in Cairo: The Basis of a Typology." *Cairo Papers in Social Sciences*, Vol. 10, Monograph 4, Cairo: AUC Press, Winter 1987.

Parker, Richard B., Robin Sabin, and Caroline Williams. *Islamic Monuments in Cairo: A Practical Guide*, 3rd ed, Cairo: AUC Press, 1985.

Rodenbeck, Max. "Draconian Powers." *The Middle East International* (24 July 1992): 11.

Rondinelli, Dennis A. *Secondary Cities in Developing Countries: Policies for Diffusing Urbanization*, Beverly Hills, CA: Sage Publications, 1983.

Rushdy, Hatem J. "The Disinherited." *Cairo Today* (February 1992): 74–76, 107.

Russell, Dorothea. *Medieval Cairo and the Monasteries of Wadi Natrun: A Historical Guide*, London, Weidenfield and Nicolson, 1962.

Sadat, Jehan. *A Woman of Egypt*, New York: Simon & Schuster, 1987.

Samir, Abeer. "No Respect for Child Labor Laws." *The Middle East Times* (20–26 October 1992): 10.

Samy, Ahmed. "Death of the City of the Dead." *Transit Egypt* (Spring 1993): 5.

Saqqaf, Abdulaziz Y. (ed). *The Middle East City, Ancient Traditions Confront a Modern World*, New York: Paragon House Publishers, 1987.

Stephen, Angela. "In the Arms of the Law." *Cairo Today* (February 1992): 70–73, 106.

United States Agency for International Development. *USAID Egypt Country Program Strategy 1992–1996 Report*, May 1992.

Wallace, Wendy. "Avoiding Traffic Jams." *The Middle East* (March 1992): 5.

"Warning Shots." *The Economist* (October 31–November 6, 1992): 46.

Watson, Helen. *Women in the City of the Dead*, Trenton, NJ: Africa World Press, 1992.

Weil, Tom. *The Cemetery Book: Graveyards, Catacombs and Other Travel Haunts*, New York: Hippocrone Books, 1992.

Weit, Gaston (translation by Seymour Feiler). *Cairo: City of Art & Commerce*, Norman, Oklahoma: University of Oklahoma Press, 1964.

Wikan, Unni (translation by Ann Henning). *Life Among the Poor in Cairo*, London: Tavistock Publications, 1980.

INDEX

Abbass, Mamdouh, 59, 69, 73, 84–92
Abbassid Caliphs, 18–19
Abu-Lughod, Janet, 3, 14, 27, 65, 99
Abu Taleb, Ali ibn, 15
Ahmed, Fardoos, 108–13
Akher, Governor Omar Abdel, 97–99, 102
Ali, Fatima, 37–39
'Ali, Muhammad, 26
Ali, Zeinab, 28–33
'Amr, 'Ogba ibn, 15
Arabe ("His Generation"), 81–84
Arabs, conquest of Egypt, 6, 12–15, 115
art historians, 99, 102
al-As, 'Amr ibn, 12
'Atika, Sayyida, 16
Aybak, 19
al-Ayyubi, Salah al-Din, 3, 13–14, 18
Ayyubids, 13–14, 18–19

Bab al-Nasr Cemetery, 3, 98, 103–13
Bab al-Wazir Cemetery, 4, 24
Barquq, Sultan, 22–23, 25, 45, 66

Barsbay, Sultan, 23, 33
birth control, 62. *See also* women
borrowing, 60
British occupation, 6, 22, 27
burial practices, 5, 13, 85, 116

Cairo, 2, 5, 7, 11, 14, 16, 41–42, 46, 48–50, 98, 115–16
Cairo: 1001 Years of the City Victorious, 3, 14, 27, 65, 99
caretakers, 4, 11, 43, 52
cemeteries, attitudes toward, 6, 26–27, 120–22
Cemetery of the Great, 3, 13–19, 45, 78, 98
child labor, 61, 64, 64 n, 66, 71
children, 31, 61–65
Christians, 12
circumcision, 64, 64 n, 74. *See also* female circumcision
Citadel, 3–4, 19, 24
Copts, 12
courtship, 73, 111. *See also* marriage
crime, 37, 80, 81, 117

criminals, 11, 43
Crusaders, 19–20

al-Dawadar, Yunus, 25
democratic values, 121
De Soto, Hernando, 45, 50
al-Din, Salah (al-Ayyubi). *See* al-Ayyubi, Salah al-Din
discrimination, 75–76
door-sitting, 36, 56–58
drugs, 76–77, 80
al-Durr, Shagar, 19

economics, 7–8, 57, 65–67, 70–72, 117, 119
education, 28, 31, 47–48, 63, 78, 119
employment, 65–66, 117, 119; and women, 60
empowerment, 120

family: life, 51, 54–65; visits, 4, 74–75
Fandy, Mamoun, 49
Fatima, daughter of the Prophet, 15–17
Fatimids, 13, 15–18
female circumcision, 64, 74
French occupation, 6, 26
al-Fustat, 15–16

al-Ga'fari, Muhammad, 16
gossip, 36
government plans, 7, 97–99, 103, 117
al-Guyushi, Amr, 16

al-Hakim, Sayyid Mohamed 'Abd, 13
health care, 47, 63 n, 68–70, 119
housing crisis, 2, 14, 27, 47, 116
housing legislation, 42
Howsh al-Basha, 26

Imbabi, Zekia, 33–37
Inal, Sultan, 21–22

informal housing, 41–48, 116, 118; definition of, 46
infrastructure, 4, 43–44, 49, 52, 67–68, 78, 82, 84–85, 94, 118
Islamic militancy, 64, 76–77, 103, 117; Jamaat Islamiya, 77; Muslim Brotherhood, 77
Islamic scholars, 99, 102

Jamaat Islamiya, 77

al-Kalawati, Shahin, 25–26
al-Kebir, 'Ali Bey, 14
key money, 52

li-Din Allah, Caliph al-Mu'izz, 15
al-Lyth, Imam, 21

madrasa, 6, 14, 23, 24
Mahfouz, Naguib, 54, 76
Mamlukes, 13, 19–26, 33, 116; Bahri, 20; Burgi, 20, 22, 25
markets, 67
marriage, 17, 29, 34, 53, 58, 60, 71, 73, 89, 90, 111; average age of, 53; concept of, 58–59; conflict, 90–91; courtship, 73, 111
Martyr's Cemetery, 53
men, 54–55, 69, 78–90; dress, 54–55; social activities, 54
migrants. *See* rural-to-urban migrants
mihrab, 5, 14, 17–18
minarets, 16, 24
Mohamed ("Life, Politics and Sophia Loren"), 92–95
Mohamed, Ashrof, 78–81
Mohamed, Salah, 104–6
monasteries, 20–21
monks, 11, 21, 116
Moquattam Hills, 3, 11, 16, 25
mosques, 6, 67; of Amir Qurqumas al-Kabir, 23; of Imam al-Shafi'i, 14; of Sayyida Nafisa, 17–18, 73;

of Sultan Barquq, 53; of Sultan Inal, 23; of Sultan Qaytbay, 24
Mousa, Mohamed, 106–8
Mubarak, President Hosni, 61, 98
Muhammad, Prophet, 5, 13, 16–17, 24, 72
Muhammad, Sultan-An Nasser, 21
mulid, 14, 72–73, 95
Muslim Brotherhood, 77

Nafisa, Sayyida, 17, 45, 72–73, 75, 92
Northern Cemetery, 3, 21–24, 35, 45, 76, 78, 80, 82

opposition (to government plans), 99–103
The Other Path, 45, 50
Ottomans, 6, 20, 25–26

poor, 11, 14–15, 42–43, 75, 77, 115–16; definitions of, 8
prayer niches, 5, 14, 17–18
Prophet Muhammad, 5, 13, 16–17, 24, 72

al-Qahira, 16
Qaytbay, Sultan, 22, 24, 45, 66, 78
Qu'ran, 5; reciters of the, 11, 43, 116
Qurqumas, Amir, 23

Ramadan, 5, 74
reciters, 11, 43, 116
religion, 72–75
religious festivals, 5, 14, 72–73, 94
Ruqaya, Sayyida, 17
rural life, 51; marriage in, 58; women in, 55
rural-to-urban migrants, 47–51, 78, 81–82, 116, 119

Sadat, Jehan, 49–50, 74
el-Saftey, Dr. Nadia, 74–75

schools, 14, 23–24, 70, 116. *See also* education
al-Shafi'i, Imam, 13–15, 17, 26, 45, 67, 72
Shehata, Governor Abdel-Rehim, 97
Shi'i Islam, 14, 16–17
sick, the, 11, 14–15, 43, 75, 116
al-Siqilly, General Gawhar, 15
Southern Cemetery, 3, 12–19, 21, 26, 67
spiritual blessing, 14, 17
Sufis, 11, 21–22, 116
Sultan, Inal, 21–22
Sultan Barquq, 22–23, 25, 45, 66
Sultan Barsbay, 23, 33
Sultan Qaytbay, 22, 24, 45, 66, 78
Sunni Islam, 13–14, 16–18, 72

tomb-keepers, 4, 43, 52, 65
tomb owners, 99, 101–2
Tughay, Princess, 21
Tulbay, Princess, 21
Tulunids, 13
Turan Shah, 19

unemployment, 41, 65, 76, 119
USAID (United States Agency for International Development), 42, 47, 63
utilities, 36, 45, 47, 49, 78, 94

War, 39, 52; 1973 War, 39; 1967 War, 52; World Wars, 27
War Cemetery, 39, 53
Watson, Helen, 55, 59
women, 28–39, 55–61; birth control, 62; borrowing, 60; door-sitting, 36, 56–58; dress, 56; education, 28, 71; gossiping, 36; work, 60

al-Yusufi, Mangak, 24

zabaleen, 68

About the Author

JEFFREY A. NEDOROSCIK has lived and worked in Egypt since 1992. He studied the City of the Dead as a Thomas J. Watson Fellow. He currently works as a contractor for the United States Agency for International Development and recently received a Sasakawa Peace Foundation fellowship to study violent internal conflict in underdeveloped nations.

HARDCOVER BAR CODE